Quod scriptura, non iubet vetat

The Latin translates, "What is not commanded in scripture, is forbidden:'

On the Cover: Baptists rejoice to hold in common with other evangelicals the main principles of the orthodox Christian faith. However, there are points of difference and these differences are significant. In fact, because these differences arise out of God's revealed will, they are of vital importance. Hence, the barriers of separation between Baptists and others can hardly be considered a trifling matter. To suppose that Baptists are kept apart solely by their views on Baptism or the Lord's Supper is a regrettable misunderstanding. Baptists hold views which distinguish them from Catholics, Congregationalists, Episcopalians, Lutherans, Methodists, Pentecostals, and Presbyterians, and the differences are so great as not only to justify, but to demand, the separate denominational existence of Baptists. Some people think Baptists ought not teach and emphasize their differences but as E.J. Forrester stated in 1893, "Any denomination that has views which justify its separate existence, is bound to promulgate those views. If those views are of sufficient importance to justify a separate existence, they are important enough to create a duty for their promulgation ... the very same reasons which justify the separate existence of any denomination make it the duty of that denomination to teach the distinctive doctrines upon which its separate existence rests." If Baptists have a right to a separate denominational life, it is their duty to propagate their distinctive principles, without which their separate life cannot be justified or maintained.

Many among today's professing Baptists have an agenda to revise the Baptist distinctives and redefine what it means to be a Baptist. Others don't understand why it even matters. The books being reproduced in the *Baptist Distinctives Series* are republished in order that Baptists from the past may state, explain and defend the primary Baptist distinctives as they understood them. It is hoped that this Series will provide a more thorough historical perspective on what it means to be distinctively Baptist.

The Lord Jesus Christ asked, *"And why call ye me, Lord, Lord, and do not the things which I say?"* (Luke 6:46). The immediate context surrounding this question explains what it means to be a true disciple of Christ. Addressing the same issue, Christ's question is meant to show that a confession of discipleship to the Lord Jesus Christ is inconsistent and untrue if it is not accompanied with a corresponding submission to His authoritative commands. Christ's question teaches us that a true recognition of His authority as Lord inevitably includes a submission to the authority of His Word. Hence, with this question Christ has made it forever impossible to separate His authority as King from the authority of His Word. These two principles—the authority of Christ as King and the authority of His Word—are the two most fundamental Baptist distinctives. The first gives rise to the second and out of these two all the other Baptist distinctives emanate. As F.M. Iams wrote in 1894, "Loyalty to Christ as King, manifesting itself in a constant and unswerving obedience to His will as revealed in His written Word, is the real source of all the Baptist distinctives:' In the search for the *primary* Baptist distinctive many have settled on the Lordship of Christ as the most basic distinctive. Strangely, in doing this, some have attempted to separate Christ's Lordship from the authority of Scripture, as if you could embrace Christ's authority without submitting to what He commanded. However, while Christ's Lordship and Kingly authority can be isolated and considered essentially for discussion's sake, we see from Christ's own words in Luke 6:46 that His Lordship is really inseparable from His Word and, with regard to real Christian discipleship, there can be no practical submission to the one without a practical submission to the other.

In the symbol above the Kingly Crown and the Open Bible represent the inseparable truths of Christ's Kingly and Biblical authority. The Crown and Bible graphics are supplemented by three Bible verses (Ecclesiastes 8:4, Matthew 28:18-20, and Luke 6:46) that reiterate and reinforce the inextricable connection between the authority of Christ as King and the authority of His Word. The truths symbolized by these components are further emphasized by the Latin quotation - *quod scriptura, non iubet vetat*— *i.e.,* "What is not commanded in scripture, is forbidden:' This Latin quote has been considered historically as a summary statement of the regulative principle of Scripture. Together these various symbolic components converge to exhibit the two most foundational Baptist Distinctives out of which all the other Baptist Distinctives arise. Consequently, we have chosen this composite symbol as a logo to represent the primary truths set forth in the *Baptist Distinctives Series*.

IMMERSION,

THE ACT OF CHRISTIAN BAPTISM

JOHN T. CHRISTIAN
1854-1925

IMMERSION,

THE ACT OF CHRISTIAN BAPTISM

BY

JOHN T. CHRISTIAN, A.M., D.D.,

Corresponding Secretary of the Convention Board of Mississippi Baptists

With a Biographical Sketch of the Author by John Franklin Jones

FOURTH THOUSAND.

LOUISVILLE, KY.
BAPTIST BOOK CONCERN
1891

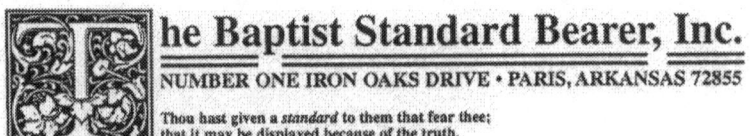

The Baptist Standard Bearer, Inc.
NUMBER ONE IRON OAKS DRIVE • PARIS, ARKANSAS 72855

Thou hast given a *standard* to them that fear thee;
that it may be displayed because of the truth.
-- Psalm 60:4

Reprinted 2006

by

THE BAPTIST STANDARD BEARER, INC.
No. 1 Iron Oaks Drive
Paris, Arkansas 72855
(479) 963-3831

THE WALDENSIAN EMBLEM
lux lucet in tenebris
"The Light Shineth in the Darkness"

ISBN# 157978416X

PREFACE.

THIS book is the result of long and patient investigation. It was with a view of satisfying the author's own mind that these studies were begun, and with no intention of writing a book. Many large libraries have been gone over, and a somewhat extensive correspondence conducted. Many of the books quoted are exceedingly rare, and many more locked up in foreign languages, and it occurred to me that these authorities might be of service to those who have neither the time nor opportunity to investigate so large a range of literature.

I am under obligation to many friends who have assisted me in divers ways. I cordially mention my lifelong friend, Prof. Arthur Yager, Ph. D., of Georgetown College, Ky. He was especially helpful in translating French and German authors. And I am indebted to Rev. Basil Manly, D. D., LL. D., of the Southern Baptist Theological Seminary, for suggestions in Hebrew and Syriac.

This book has been written in no controversial spirit, and it is given to the public with a sincere desire to do good. That it is not faultless the author is well aware, but he does believe that the propositions laid down are in accord with the Holy Scriptures, and in harmony with the universal teachings of history.

CONTENTS.

	PAGE.
CHAPTER I. The Law of Baptism and Principles of Interpretation.	7
CHAPTER II. What the Lexicons say	16
CHAPTER III. What the Classical Writers say	23
CHAPTER IV. Does Baptizo Necessarily Mean to Drown?	31
CHAPTER V, What the Septuagint says	36
CHAPTER VI. The Baptism of John	46
CHAPTER VII. The Baptism of Jesus	56
CHAPTER VIII. The Baptism Mentioned in Mark vii: 1–4	63
CHAPTER IX. The Baptism of the Three Thousand	71
CHAPTER X. The Baptism of the Ethiopian Eunuch	83
CHAPTER XI. Paul's Baptism	89
CHAPTER XII. The Baptism of the Jailer	94
CHAPTER XIII. The Argument from Rom. vi: 4	102
CHAPTER XIV. What the Greek Fathers say	108

CONTENTS.

CHAPTER XV.
What the Latin Fathers say........................ 114

CHAPTER XVI.
"The Teaching of the Twelve Apostles"............. 119

CHAPTER XVII.
Argument from History in favor of Immersion....... 128

CHAPTER XVIII.
Sprinkling a Heathen Custom........................ 136

CHAPTER XIX.
The Baptism of the Sick............................ 151

CHAPTER XX.
The History of Sprinkling.......................... 158

CHAPTER XXI.
What the Councils of the Roman Catholic Church say. 167

CHAPTER XXII.
The Testimony of the Liturgies and Rituals.......... 176

CHAPTER XXIII.
What the Poets say................................. 182

CHAPTER XXIV.
What the Greek Church says......................... 192

CHAPTAR XXV.
What the Catholic Church says...................... 204

CHAPTER XXVI.
What the Episcopalians say......................... 213

CHAPTER XXVII.
What the Presbyterians say......................... 223

CHAPTER XXVIII.
What the Methodists say............................ 233

CHAPTER XXIX.
What the Syriac says............................... 240

IMMERSION.

CHAPTER I.

THE LAW OF BAPTISM, AND THE PRINCIPLES OF INTERPRETATION.

THE law of baptism is laid down in Matthew xxviii: 18–20, in the words of our Saviour: "All power is given unto me in heaven and in earth. Go ye, therefore, and teach all nations, baptizing them in the name of the Father, and of the Son, and of the Holy Ghost; teaching them to observe all things whatsoever I have commanded you: and, lo, I am with you alway, even unto the end of the world. Amen."

The terms of this commission are plain enough. I shall apply some of the principles of constitutional and statutory law to the law of baptism; and in it will be found an unanswerable argument in favor of immersion. Greenleaf, a very able lawyer, applied the principles of law to the Four Gospels, and gave to the world one of the strongest books on Christian Evidence extant; and I am sure that from the same standpoint the argument for immersion is impregnable.

I shall call attention to a few of the fundamental principles of law:

1. Words are to be used in their primary or historical sense, and in the meaning in which they can be proven historically to have been used. No secondary or figurative sense can be applied to words as long as the historical sense can be applied to them. This is a fundamental rule, and is laid down in all of the law books.

Blackstone, on the interpretation of law, says: "Words are generally to be understood in their usual and most known signification; not so much regarding the propriety of grammar, as their general and popular use." (Com. 59.) Greenleaf says: "The terms of every written instrument are to be understood in their plain, ordinary and popular sense." (On Evid. 278.)

This idea is as applicable to theology as it is to law. So clear is this that the celebrated Presbyterian author, Dr. Charles Hodge, says: "The fundamental interpretation of all writings, sacred and profane, is that words are to be understood in their historical sense in which it can be historically proved that they were used by their authors, and intended to be understood by those to whom they were addressed. The object of language is the communication of thought. Unless words are taken in the sense in which those who employ them know they will be understood, they will fail of their design." (Systemat. Theol., vol. 1, p. 376.)

If this rule holds good, immersion is inevitably the act of Christian baptism. Beyond doubt the historical sense of the word *baptizo* is to dip. Even if it could be proven, which is not the case, that some tropical definition favored affusion, still, with this rule in sight, baptism logically would be performed by immersion. We have no right to give the word an arbitrary meaning. This principle is recognized in the interpretation of all law; why not in the law of baptism?

2. We have no right to put any arbitrary construction upon, or to draw any strained inference from, the law of baptism. The New Testament is to be construed plainly, and from its express commands there can be no departure.

Upon no point is the law more explicit than upon this. "*A verbis legis non est recedendum:* from the words of the law there can be no departure. A court of law will not make any interpretation contrary to the express letter of the statute; for nothing can so well explain the meaning of the makers of the Act as their own direct words." (Brown, 622.) "When a law is plain and unambiguous, whether it be expressed in general or limited terms, the legislators should be interpreted to mean what they have plainly expressed, and consequently no room is left for construction. Possible or probable meanings, where one is plainly declared in the instrument itself, the courts are not at liberty to search for elsewhere." . . . "That which the words declare is the meaning of the instrument, neither courts nor legislators have a right to add to or take away from its meaning." (On Constit. Lim. 68, 70.) Mr. Cooly continues: "In the case of all written laws it is the intent of the lawgiver that it is to be enforced. But this intent is to be found in the instrument itself. It is to be presumed that language has been employed with sufficient precision to convey it, and, unless examination demonstrates that the presumption holds good in the particular case, nothing will remain except to enforce it." (Constit. Lim. 68.) Mr. Marshall, Chief Justice of the United States, said: "The government of the United States can claim no powers which are not granted to it by the Constitution; and the powers actually granted must be such as are expressly given, or given by necessary implication." (1 Wheat. 326, Brown.) "The intention of the testator ought to be the only guide of the court to the interpretation of his will; yet it must be his intention, as collected by the words employed by himself in his will. No surmise or conjecture of any object, which the testator may be supposed to have had in view, can be allowed to have any weight in the construction of his will unless such object be collected from the plain language of the will itself." (555.)

These writers all say that from the words of the law there must be no departure. Now this is perfectly evident. If this commission of Christ means immersion, we can not depart from the letter and allow any other act. If it were "possible," or "even probable," that sprinkling or pouring was the act of baptism, yet they could not be admitted, since immersion is "the historical or primary" sense of the word *baptizo*. No room is left for construction, and we are to take the Scriptures just as they read. We are not to read meanings into the word of the living God.

3. If the commission is not perfectly plain and explicit in all of its terms it is of no binding force whatever. This the law books plainly teach. The maxim is, *ubi jus incertum, ubi jus nullum*, when the law is uncertain, there is no law. The learned Judge Pothier says: "A law that is hopelessly obscure is of no binding force, and no person can be held responsible for obedience to it." Greenleaf remarks: "In other words, in merely gener-

ally speaking, if the court, placing itself in the situation in which the testator or contracting party stood at the time of executing the instrument, and with full understanding of the force and import of the words, cannot ascertain his meaning and intention from the language of the instrument thus illustrated, it is a case of incurable and hopeless uncertainty, and the instrument is so far inoperative and void." (On Evid. 300.)

Jesus Christ can claim no authority that is not expressed in his commands; and it would be a reflection to say that he did not make himself perfectly clear. If no man can tell what the commission means, or if it means any one of a dozen things, then is baptism not binding upon us. But such a proposition is at once sacrilegious and absurd.

4. The expression of one thing is the exclusion of another. If immersion is expressed, then is sprinkling and pouring excluded. There is "one baptism," and not three. Coke says: "The appointment or designation of one is the exclusion of another; and that expressed makes that which is implied to cease." (Coke-Lit. 210.) And Brown says: "If authority is given expressly, though by affirmative words, upon a defined condition, the expression of that condition excludes the doing of

the act authorized under other circumstances than those so defined." (653.)

Unquestionably the Scriptures teach that baptism is by immersion, and affusion is thus rejected by this law of exclusion.

5. It would be of no service to us if Christ had commanded us to be baptized, if we could not know what he meant. Mr. Coke says: "It avails little to know what ought to be done, if you do not know how it is to be done." "Where any thing," says Brown, "is commanded, every thing by which it is to be accomplished is also commanded." (482.) Certainly there would be no doubt thrown around the last command the Son of God ever gave.

6. Next to the authority of the New Testament, which is paramount, the admissions of learned Pedobaptists is the strongest proof we can possibly offer. The admission of the adverse party, when deliberately made, is the strongest authority in a court of law. The principle is the same whether applied to civil or criminal matters. Starkie and Greenleaf both put this proposition in the strongest terms. Greenleaf says: "It is generally agreed that deliberate confessions of guilt are among the most effectual proofs of the law. Their value depends on the supposition that they are deliberate

and voluntary, and on the presumption that a rational being will not make admissions prejudicial to his interest and safety, unless when urged by the promptings of truth and conscience. Such confessions, so made by a prisoner, at any moment of time, and at any place, subsequent to the perpetration of crime, and previous to his examination before the magistrate, are at common law received in evidence as among proofs of guilt." (On Evid. 215.)

There can be but one conclusion in regard to the hundreds of Pedobaptist scholars who have admitted that baptism was originally by immersion. The truth forced them to this conclusion. I emphasize this fundamental principle of the law of evidence, that the admissions of the adverse party, against his interest or opinion, is the best of evidence in law, and is an estoppel in the controversy. I claim that the admissions of the best pedobaptist scholars of this and every other age, forever close out affusion as baptism.

The law requires absolute obedience, and we have no right to change or in any wise alter its demands. No crime is greater than disobedience." (Jenks, Cent. Car. 77.) "Obedience is the essence of the law." (11 Coke 100.) Obedience is the crowning grace of all. It is that "principle, I mean, to which Polity owes its stability, Life its happiness, Faith its acceptance, Creation its continuance." This is the principle that recognizes the well nigh forgotten truth that Christ is Lord as well as Saviour. It is a far reaching truth, and strict obedience to it carries us into the immediate presence of God. No more significant words are in the Bible than those of Jesus Christ, "Ye are my friends, if ye do whatsoever I have commanded you."

CHAPTER II.

WHAT THE LEXICONS SAY.

WHEN we desire the definition of a word we naturally turn to a dictionary, or lexicon, for its meaning. This I now do. I present only such authorities as I have before me; and take no statement at second hand. These writers are certainly competent witnesses. These Greek lexicons were not written by Baptists, but by Pedobaptist scholars. As Mr. Greenfield expressed it: "I wish it to be distinctly understood that I am neither a Baptist, nor the son of a Baptist; nor is it my business to make a defense of their cause."

Sometime since I wrote Dr. Gross Alexander, Professor of New Testament Exegesis in Vanderbilt, the great Methodist University of the South, asking him kindly to mention two Greek lexicons—one on Classical and the other on the New Testament Greek, that he regarded as the very best. He wrote by return mail, in reply: "The *seventh* edition of Liddell and Scott, Harper & Bros., N. Y., is the *best* Greek lexicon for general use. I emphasize *seventh*; for as compared with former editions it is a new book. The very best New Testament lexicon is that of J. H. Thayer, Greek-English lexicon, published also by Harper & Bros."

Dr. C. C. Hersman, President of the Southwestern Presbyterian University, at Clarksville, Tenn., writes me under date of Aug. 7th, 1890. He says: "In English the best Classical Greek lexicon is Liddell and Scott, the last edition. It is based on the great work of Passow. In the New Testament nothing can compare with the lexicon of J. H. Thayer based on Grimm-Wilkes *Clavis Novi Testamenti*. Robinson's is a very good one. But Thayer, when used with caution and intelligence, is *par excellence*. He gives the very latest results."

No name among Presbyterians outranks that of C. W. Hodge, Professor of New Testament Criticism in Princeton Theological Seminary. He writes, Aug. 10th, 1890, as follows: "The best Classical Greek lexicon is Liddell and Scott's. The best New Testament Lexicon is Thayer's edition of Grimm."

No scholar is likely to dissent from these opinions. Liddell and Scott are learned Episcopalian scholars of England. I turn to the seventh edition, the one all of these scholars say is the best, p. 274, and *baptizo* is defined, "to dip in or under water." Not a word is said about sprinkling or pouring. That witness is satisfactory enough.

Prof. J. H. Thayer, the author of the Greek-English Lexicon of the New Testament, is Prof. of New Testament Criticism and Interpretation, in the Divinity School of Harvard University, Cambridge, Mass. On p. 94, I read: "*Baptizo*, to dip repeatedly, to immerse, to submerge. In the New Testament it is used particularly of the rite of sacred ablution, first instituted by John the Baptist, afterward by Christ's command received by Christians and adjusted to the nature and contents of their religion, viz: an immersion in water." Under *baptisma* he says, "a word peculiar to the N. T. and ecclesiastical writers, immersion, submersion."

To make assurance doubly sure and leave not a hook to hang a doubt upon I give the testimony of other lexicons.

Prof. E. A. Sophocles, a native Greek, and for thirty-eight years Professor of Greek in Harvard University, in his lexicon of Greek usages in the Roman and Byzantine periods, B. C. 146– A. D. 1100, Boston 1887, defines *baptizo*, "to dip, to immerse, to sink. There is no evidence that Luke and Paul and the other writers of the New Testament put upon this verb meanings not recognized by the Greeks."

J. W. Fradensdorf, of the Taylor Institute, in

WHAT THE LEXICONS SAY.

his English-Greek Lexicon, London 1860, defines *baptizein* and *baptein* "to baptize, to dip."

Dr. W. Pope, of the Berlin Gymnasium, 1842, 1870, 1880, defines *baptizo*, "to dip in, to dip under."

Wahl, Clavis, Leipzig 1853, says: "*Baptizo*, to dip, to dip repeatedly, to immerse, to wash."

E. W. Bullinger, Greek Lexicon and Concordance, London 1878, p. 81, says: "*Baptizo*, to make a thing dipped or dyed, to immerse for a religious purpose. By baptism therefore we must understand an immersion, whose design, like that of the levitical washings and purifications, was united with the washing away of sin."

Cremer, Biblico-Theological Greek Lexicon of the New Testament, third English edition, 1883, p. 126: "*baptizo*, to immerse, to submerge. The peculiar New Testament and Christian use of the word to denote immersion, submersion for a religious purpose—baptize."

Ab. H. Stephanus, Thesaurus Græcæ Linguæ, London 1821, vol. 3, p. 20,681, "*baptizo*, to merge, to immerse, also to dip."

Hedericus, Lexicon, London, 1755, "*baptizo*, to merge, to immerse, to wash in water."

Bass, London 1859, p. 39, "*baptizo*, to dip, immerse, or plunge in water. 2nd. To baptize figuratively, to be immersed in suffering or affliction."

Suicer, Thesaurus, Amsterdam 1682, p. 622, "*baptizo*, to immerse, to dip."

Scapula, Genevæ 1628, p. 254, "*baptizo*, to merge, to immerse; also, dye, as we immerse things for the purpose of coloring or washing them. Also to immerse, to submerge, to wash in water."

Stokius, Clavis, Leipzig 1752, "*baptizo*, by the **force** of the word indicates the idea of dipping or immersion   Properly speaking it is a dipping or an immersion in water."

Schoettgenius, Greek Lexicon, Lugudi, Balavorum, 1755, p. 107, "*baptizo*, 1st, properly to dip, to immerse; 2nd, to bathe, to wash."

Schleusner, Glasgow, vol. 1, p. 338, "*baptizo*, properly to immerse, to dip, to immerse in water."

Schrevelius, "*baptizo*, to baptize, to dip."

Simonis, Halæ, 1766, "*baptizo*, to dip."

Green, "*baptizo*, to dip, to immerse."

Greenfield, "*baptizo*, to immerse, to immerge, to submerge, to sink."

Donnegan, "*baptizo*, to immerse repeatedly in a liquid, to submerge."

Groves, "*baptizo*, to dip, to immerse, to immerge, to plunge."

Robinson, "*baptizo*, to dip in, to sink, to immerse."

G. P. Lascarides, London 1882, p. 341, "*baptizo,* to dip."

Here is the testimony of twenty-four Greek lexicons; and every one of them gives the primary idea of dipping. I have at hand the testimony of three living American Bishops, who, while they hold to affusion on other accounts, allow dipping to be the primary meaning of the word. Bishop John J. Keane, President of the Catholic University of America, Washington, D. C., says: "The best dictionaries show the classical meaning of the Greek word *baptizein* is primarily to plunge, to dip." Henry C. Potter, Episcopal Bishop of New York, says: "I am quite free to say that the literal meaning of *baptizo* as ordinarily found in classical writers is, usually to plunge, to dip, immerse, or whatever word you want to strengthen your position." The next is Bishop A. Cleveland Coxe, the editor of the American edition of the Ante-Nicene Fathers, who says: "The word means to dip."

We can therefore say in the none too strong language of Moses Stuart, the late eminent Congregational scholar of Andover, "*bapto* and *baptizo* mean to dip, to plunge, to immerge, into any thing liquid. All lexicographers and critics of any note are agreed in this." (On Bap., p. 51.) I have here quoted Methodist, Episcopal, Catholic, Presbyterian, and many other authorities. All these lexicons give dipping as the primary meaning; and if the word has any secondary meaning it is in accordance with this idea. The dictionaries are, therefore, all in favor of dipping as the primary meaning of this word.

CHAPTER III.

WHAT THE CLASSICAL WRITERS SAY.

AN appeal can always be made from the lexicons to the use of the word in the best authors. I now appeal to the classical Greek authors. I shall not discuss *bapto*, but confine myself to *baptizo*, the word used for baptize in the New Testament. I shall begin with the oldest writer who used this word, and, in chronological order, give the statement of writers covering several hundred years. This is the philological order, and if the word means to sprinkle or pour, we will certainly find that passage. I shall give later the testimony of the Greek fathers; here I only refer to the use of the word in the classics. There is no higher authority than this.

Pindar, B. C. 522: "For as when the rest of the tackle is toiling deep in the sea, I as a cork, above the net, am undipped (*abaptistos*) in water."

Plato, B. C. 429: "I perceiving that the youth was overwhelmed (*baptizomenon*), wishing to give him respite," etc. "I was one of those who yesterday were overwhelmed in wine."

The Homeric Allegories, B. C. 400: "The mass

of iron, drawn red hot from the furnace, is dipped (*baptizetai*) in water."

Alcibiades, B. C. 400: "You dipped (*baptes*) me in plays: but I in the waves of the sea dipping (*baptizon*), will destroy thee with streams more bitter."

Demosthenes, B. C. 385: "Not the speakers, for these know how to play the dipping (*diabaptizesthai*) match with him, but the inexperienced."

Eubulus, B. C. 380: "Who now the fourth day is immersed (*baptizetai*), leading the famished life of a miserable mullet."

Evenus of Paros, B. C. 250: "Bacchus (the use of wine) plunges (*baptizei*) in sleep."

Polybius, B. C. 205: The enemy "made continued assaults and submerged (*ebaptizon*) many of the vessels." The vessel "being submerged (*baptizomena*) became filled with sea-water and confusion." "Even if the spear falls into the sea, it is not lost; for it is compacted of oak and pine, so that when the oaken part is immersed (*baptizomenon*) by the weight, the rest is buoyed up, and it is easily recovered." "Themselves by themselves immersed (*baptizomenoi*) and sinking in the pools."

Strabo, B. C. 60: "To one who hurls down a dart, from above into the channel, the force of the water makes so much resistance, that it is hardly

WHAT THE CLASSICAL WRITERS SAY. 25

dipped (*baptizesthai*)." "And he who enters into it is not immersed (*baptizesthai*), but is lifted out." "The water solidifies so rapidly around every thing that is dipped into it (Lake Tatta) that they draw up salt crowns when they let down a circle of rushes."

Diodorus, B. C. 60: "The river rushing down with the current increased in violence, immersed (*ebaptize*) many." "Most of the wild animals are surrounded by the stream and perished, being submerged (*baptizomena*); but some escaping to the high grounds, are saved." "His ship being submerged (*baptistheisas*)." "They do not whelm (*baptizousi*) the common people with taxes."

Conon, about A. D. 1: "Having whelmed (*baptisasa*) with much wine and put him to sleep."

Josephus, A. D. 37: "And stretching out the right hand, so as to be unseen by any, he plunged the whole sword into his body." There are thirteen other examples in Josephus all in the sense of dipping.

Philo, the Jew, A. D. 50: "The reason was whelmed (*baptizomenou*) by the things overlying it."

Plutarch, A. D. 50: "A bladder, then mayest be dipped (*baptize*); but it is not possible for thee to sink." "The soldiers along the whole way, dipping (*baptizontes*) with cups, and horns, and goblets, from great wine jars and mixing bowls, were drinking to one another." Thirteen other times is the word used in Plutarch in the sense of to dip.

Epictetus, A. D. 50: "You would not wish, sailing in a large and polished, and richly gilded ship, to be submerged (*baptizesthai*)."

Demetrius, the Sidonian, A. D. 50: "She is not wholly dipped (*bebaptisthai*), but rises above."

Alciphron, A. D. 150: "If I am to see all the rivers, life to me will be whelmed (*baptisthasetai*), not beholding Glycera."

Lucian, the man-hater, A. D. 135: "If the winter's torrent were bearing one away, and he with outstretched hands were imploring help, to thrust even him headlong, dipping (*baptizonta*), so that he should not be able to come up again." "He seems like one heavy-headed and whelmed (*bebaptismeno*)."

Polyænus, A. D. 150: "Philip did not give over dipping (*diabaptizomenos*) in a match with the pancratiast, and sprinkling (*rainomenos*) water in his face, until the soldiers, wearied out, dispersed."

Dion Cassius, A. D. 150: "And others leaping into the sea were drowned, or, struck by the enemy, were submerged (*ebaptizonto*)." There are seven other examples of dipping in this writer.

Plotinus, A. D. 205: "Death to her while yet

immersed (*bebaptismena*) in the body, is to be sunk in matter." "But now, since a part of us is contained by the body, as if one has the feet in water, but with the rest of the body stands out above, towering up by what is not immersed (*baptisthenti*) in the body, we by this are attached, as to our own center, with that which is the center of all." "He does not continue happy, whelmed (*baptistheis*) either with diseases or with arts of magicians."

Aristophen, A. D. 210: "Then whelming (*baptisas*) potently with wine, he set me free."

Porphyra, A. D. 233: "When the accused answers to it, if he is guiltless, he goes through without fear, having the water as far as to the knees; but if guilty, after proceeding a little way, he is immersed (*baptizetai*) unto the head."

Heimerius, A. D. 315: "I will show you also my soldiers; one fighting life-like even in the painting . . . and another dipping (*baptizonta*) with his hands the Persian fleet." "He was great at Salamis; for there, fighting, he whelmed (*ebaptise*) all Asia."

Libanius, A. D. 315: "I myself am one of those immersed (*baptismenon*) by that great wave." He used the word nine other times to dip.

Themistius, A. D. 375: "The pilot, whether he saves in the voyage one whom it were better to submerge (*baptisai*)." "Overwhelmed (*baptizomenon*) by grief."

The Argonautic Expedition, A. D. 375: "But when Titon dipped himself into the ocean stream."

Chariton, A. D. 375: "Overwhelmed (*baptizomenos*) by design." "Overwhelmed (*ebaptizeto*) as to the soul." "Overwhelmed (*baptizomenon*) in a calm."

Heliodorus, A.D. 390: "Already becoming dipped (*baptizomenon*), and wanting little of sinking, some of the pirates attempted to leave and get aboard of their own bark." "Slaying some on land, and plunging (*baptizonton*) others with their boats and huts into the lake." There are four other examples in Heliodorus.

Proclus, A. D. 412: "The Io-Bacchus was sung at festivals and sacrifices of Bacchus, immersed (*bebaptismenon*) with much wantonness."

Achilles Tatius, A. D. 450: "They dip (*baptizousi*) into the water, therefore, a pole smeared with pitch, and open the barriers of the stream." "They who behold suppose the steel is plunged (*baptizesthai*) down the body, but it runs back into the hollow of the hilt."

Julian, A. D. 525: "As I was once trimming a garland, I found Cupid in the roses; and holding by the wings, I dipped (*ebaptisa*) him into wine

WHAT THE CLASSICAL WRITERS SAY.

and took him and drank him, and now within my members he tickles with his wings."

Simplicius, A. D. 650: "Beauty in bodies, is in flesh and sinews and things that make up the body, of animals, for example; beautifying them, indeed, as much as possible, but also itself partaking of their deformity, and immersed (*bebaptismenon*) into it."

Eustathius, A. D. 1100: "My whole mind was overwhelmed (*katabaptistheis*) with the affliction." "My spirit thou didst overwhelm (*katebaptisas*), surging round, with whole seas of wailings." "Strives to overwhelm (*katabaptisai*) the whole vessel with the waves."

I have here quoted thirty-three authors, and have given fifty-six examples of the use of the word in these writers. These authors cover a period of over sixteen hundred years, commencing with Pindar, B. C. 522, and ending with Eustathius in the eleventh century A. D. The invariable meaning of the word in all of these passages is to dip, or some word which conveys the same idea. So clear is this that Prof. Stuart says: "It is impossible to doubt that the words *bapto* and *baptizo* have, in the Greek classical writers, the sense of dip, plunge, immerse, sink, etc." (Bap. p. 56.)

The only possible objection that can be made to this meaning is where the classical writers use such phrases as "overwhelmed in wine," "overwhelmed in sleep," "overwhelmed in sorrow," etc.; but even here the idea is an immersion. But this figure of speech is common in all languages and with almost every word. In the Latin this figure is very common. Livy says, "*Mersus vino somnoque*," or Virgil's "*Somno vinoque sepultus*," immersed or buried in wine; and Seneca speaks of the "*potatio quæ mergit*," the drink which immerses. In Shakspeare we read:

> "Who dipping all his faults in their affection's
> Mould, like the spring that turneth wood into stone,
> Convert his gyves into graces."—*Hamlet*, iv. 7.

Cowper sings of one:

> "Immersed in soft repose ambrosial."

We can therefore say without a doubt that *baptizo*, in classical writers, means to dip.

CHAPTER IV.

DOES BAPTIZO NECESSARILY MEAN TO DROWN, IN CLASSICAL GREEK?

IT is wonderful how many inventions there are to distort this simple Greek word "*dip.*" There is a theory gaining ground in many places that whenever the word is used in classical Greek, of persons, it means more than a dipping; it includes the idea of drowning, or a complete loss of life. Granting, for the sake of argument, this to be true, how could it help the cause of sprinkling? Surely the "sevenfold dipping" of Naaman, and the baptism of the thousands by John in the Jordan, was not a drowning. I have at hand the opinion of three learned professors of Greek. They have studied the Greek language and literature for years and they have found no such meaning.

The first is Prof. M. W. Humphreys, of the University of Virginia. He says:

UNIVERSITY OF VIRGINIA,
March 27, 1890.

My Dear Sir,—The term "classical Greek" is a little ambiguous. If profane literature is meant, there is certainly nothing in the theory you mention. If classical Attic prose is meant, the word is too rarely used in that to justify any such generalization. The word ordinarily has a figurative use in "classical Greek," such as overwhelm, as when a boy is flooded with questions, or a man is over head and ears in debt. But see the quotation from Hippocrates in Liddell and Scott's Lexicon.

Yours sincerely, M. W. HUMPHREYS.

Dr. J. H. Thayer, of Harvard Divinity School, is even more explicit:

CAMBRIDGE, MASS., 67 Sparks St., }
March 17, 1890.

Dear Sir,—In reply to your inquiry of the 14th inst., permit me to say that the Greek word *baptizo*, when used physically in reference to persons, often describes an experience which issues in death. But that the word *does not* always carry with it the idea of drowning or complete loss of life, is evident from many extant examples, which are to be found alike in the larger Greek lexicons and such special works as "Classic Baptism," by J. W. Dale, 1867, or "Meaning and Use of *Baptizein*," etc., by T. J. Conant, N. Y. 1864. Let it suffice to set down two: Polybius, who died before Christ, 122, in his History, bk. 3, ch. 72, sec. 4, describing the passage of soldiers through the river Febia, which had been swollen during the night by a heavy shower, says, "*mogis heos tou mastou hoi pezoi baptizomenoi, diaperosi*": *i. e.* they cross with difficulty, those on foot baptized as far as the breast. Again, Strabo, who died A. D. 24, in his Geography, bk. 14, ch. 3. sec. 9, describing the march of Alexander's army on one occasion, says, "*holan tan hameran en hudati genesthai tan poreian suneba mechri omphalon baptizomenon*": *i. e.* it happened that the whole day long the march was made in water, the men being immersed (*baptized*) up to the naval.

Figuratively, the word is used, as you are aware, of one drowned in grief, overwhelmed with care, immersed in debt, over head and ears in love, etc., etc.; and no more excludes of necessity the notion of ultimate rescue than such expressions in English do.

In short, the word, intrinsically and in the classic use, no more implies that the immersed person of necessity loses his life thereby, than when used of the rite of Christian baptism it implies the drowning of every person immersed.

Yours truly, J. HENRY THAYER.

Dr. Harnack, the greatest living Church historian, of the University of Berlin, writes under date of April 2nd, 1890: "But this meaning does not necessarily lie in the meaning of the word. One can be dipped (sunk) in the water without being drowned. The passages in which the word in reference to persons appears in the classic authors, are, so far as I know, not very numerous, so that we can not set up a constant usage."

These scholars state most positively that *baptizo* does not intrinsically mean to "drown."

Besides the two examples mentioned by Dr. Thayer, we have one in Hippocrates, to which Prof. Humphreys refers. Hippocrates describing the respiration of a patient affected with inflammation and swelling of the throat, and oppressed about the heart, says: "And she breathed as persons breathe after having been dipped, and emitted a low sound from the chest, like the so-called ventriloquist." This is certainly decisive. Josephus, in his Antiquities, bk. 15, ch. 3, 3, describing the murder of the boy, Aristobulus, who was drowned, by the command of Herod, by his companions in a swimming pool, says: "Continually pressing down and dipping (*baptizontes*) him while swimming, as if in sport, they did not desist till they had entirely suffocated him." If *baptizo* was equivalent to drowning, there would have been no necessity of repeatedly dipping him. I give only one more example, and that from Josephus also. He says of the Jews, in describing their contest with the Roman soldiers on the Sea of Galilee: "And when they ventured to come near, they suffered harm before they could inflict any, and were submerged (*ebaptizonto*) along with their vessels . . . and those of the immersed (*baptisthenton*) who raised their heads, either a missile reached or a vessel overtook." If *baptizo* meant to drown, these persons would not have raised their heads, nor would there have been any necessity that a vessel should overtake them. It is a drowning cause that demands any such subterfuge.

I close this argument with the statements of two learned German writers.

Witsius, vol. 3, p. 368, London 1785, says: "*Baptizo* is altogether something more than *epipolazein*, to float on the surface; but less than *dunein*, to go to the bottom and perish."

Fritzche, Com. on Matth. vol. 1, p. 120, Leipzig 1826, says: "Moreover, Casaubon well suggested that *dunein* means to be submerged with the design that you may perish; *epipolazein*, to float on the surface of the water; *baptizesthai*, to immerse oneself wholly, for another purpose than that you may perish. But that, in accordance with the nature of the word *baptizesthai*, baptism was then performed, not by sprinkling upon, but by submerging, is proved especially by Rom. vi: 4."

CHAPTER V.

WHAT THE SEPTUAGINT SAYS.

IN the Greek version of the Old Testament the word *baptizo* occurs only twice: "and Naaman went down and dipped himself seven times in the Jordan" (2 Kings 5: 14); and " My iniquity overwhelms (*baptizei*) me." (Isa. 21: 4.) The root word *bapto* is frequently used in the sense of to dip, and is so used seventeen times in the Old Testament. The Hebrew word that corresponds with *baptizo* is *tabhal*.

I present the testimony that *tabhal* means to dip:

1. It is so defined in the Lexicons. Gesenius, the best authority, says: "to dip, to dip in, to immerse."

Buxtorf, London ed. 1646, p. 264, says: "to dip, to dip in, to immerse."

E. Castello, Lexicon Heptaglotton, London 1669, vol. 1, p. 1462: "To dip, to dip in, to immerse (Eng. to dip or to babble). It differs from *rahats*, which means to wash a thing."

Davies, Andover 1879: "to dip in, to sink into."

Gibbs, New Haven 1832: "to dip in, immerse."

De Bernadus de Mauntfaucon, Paris 1713, Hexaplorum Orgines, vol. 1, p. 441: "to dip or to immerse."

Parkhurst, London 1823, p. 215, says: "to dip, to immerse, to plunge."

Schaff, Lugduni 1786, p. 62: "to merge, to immerse."

Stokius, Clairs, Leipzig 1653, p. 421: "to dip, to dip in, to immerse."

Schindlero, Lexicon Pentaglotton, Hanover 1612, p. 686 says: "to dip, to dip in, to immerse."

Simonis, edited by G. B. Miner: "to dip, to dip in, to immerse."

The testimony of these eleven lexicons is for dipping.

2. The *usus loquendi* of the word is in favor of dipping. *Tabhal* is translated fifteen times in King James' version by dip; plunge once; dyed once, because dyeing was done by dipping. (Gesenius, Lex. p. 358.) Only once is *tabhal* thus translated, and in this instance the reading is doubtful. Our own Milton speaks of colors dipped in heaven. Prof. Stuart refers to sixteen of these examples, and translates ten by dipping, three smearing on by dipping, two by plunge, and one by color. Luther translated sixteen times by dip, and once to dye. The Greek, German, and English translators all render *tabhal* to dip. Any person famil-

iar with the Hebrew would not fail to notice that the construction of *tabhal* is totally different from any word which means to sprinkle or to pour, and is followed by a different class of prepositions. It usually takes the accusative with the preposition *b,* in. Besides, the Hebrew has words meaning to sprinkle and to pour, but they are never used interchangeably with *tabhal.*

There is another word in the Hebrew Bible of kindred signification to *tabhal.* It is the Chaldee *tabhal.* The Jerusalem Targum, Jonathan's Paraphrase, and Onkelos all use it in the sense of to dip; and in the Jerusalem Targum it translates *tabhal* in Lev. iv: 6. It appears in Dan. iv: 33, and v: 31, where Nebuchadnezzar was "wet with the dew of heaven." It is defined by Gesenius, "to sink, to press in." The primary syllable *tbh* in the Western languages expresses depth and immersion (p. 353). The Greek in these passages is *bapto,* to dip. The idea is that the dew was so copious that the king was as wet as if he had been dipped. Any one who has read English literature will often find this idea. Turn to Milton's Comus, line 814:

"A cold shuddering dew dips me all over."

John Wesley, in speaking of an anxious sinner, says: "On Thursday he wrestled with God till he was wet all over with sweat as if he had been dipped in water." (Journal, vol. 2, p. 152.) And Webster gives as a definition of the word "wet," to dip or to soak in liquor.

There are three other Hebrew words in as many different passages which are translated by *bapto* and *baptizo*, but as they have not the same root I will briefly notice them. Lev. xi: 32: "The unclean thing must be put into water (*baphasetai*), and it shall be unclean until the evening." The Hebrew is *habha*, and is defined by Gesenius, "to hide, to conceal." The thing is hid in water, and hence dipped. Ps. lxviii: 23: "That thy foot may be dipped (*bapta*) in the blood of thine enemies, and the tongue of thy dogs in the same." The Hebrew is *mahats*. The Lexicons translate this passage as the English version has done. The same root is found in "depths of the sea," in verse 22d. Isa. xxi: 4: "My heart panteth, fearfulness affrighted me." The Hebrew *bi'th* is translated by the Greek *baptizei*, to dip. Stuart renders, "My iniquity overwhelms me." The idea is that he was overwhelmed by terror.

3. I shall refer to some examples taken from the Talmud—later Jewish writers than the Bible. It will be seen that *tabhal* is invariably used in the sense of to dip, or to cover over with water.

"A vessel must be dipped to render it ceremonially clean" (folio 75).

"The child of a heathen shall be dipped (*tabhal*), according to the decision of the Sanhedrim." (Treatise Chetubeth, f. 11.)

"No one is to be considered a proselyte until he be circumcised and dipped (*tabhal*); he is to be considered as a heathen."

The Talmud Tract Repuduu, speaking of Jethro, Moses' father-in-law, says: "He was made a proselyte by circumcision and immersion in water."

Rabbi Judah Hadzodesh, A. D. 220, says: "As to a proselyte, who becomes a proselyte in the evening of the passover, the followers of Shammai say, Let him be dipped (*tabhal*) and let him eat the passover in the evening." (Tract Pheshuim cviii, s. 8.)

According to the Jerusalem Talmud, Tract Pesah, Eliazer, the son of Jacob, is represented as saying "that some Roman soldiers who kept guard at Jerusalem, at the passover, being dipped (*tabhal*) in the evening of the passover."

To discuss the subject of proselyte baptism referred to above is no part of my object. That baptism was by dipping, and expressed by the Hebrew *tabhal*, to cite authorities for this purpose is needless.

That the washing of the Jews was an immersion,

does not admit of a doubt. The facts all point that way. "From an early period," says the Encyclopædia Britannica, 9th ed. vol. 3, p. 434, "the Jews bathed in running water, used both hot and cold baths, and employed oils and ointments."

Dr. Hibbard, the well known Methodist writer, says: "Within this climate lies the land of Palestine. It is such a climate as originated the demand for baths and pools and fountains throughout the East, and made the practice of bathing to be common; and we repeat it, it was this universal custom of bathing—a custom so indispensable to pleasure, to decency, to health among the Orientals—which, more than anything else, gave a bias to their minds to immersion instead of affusion." (Hibbard on Bapt. P. 2, p. 152.)

4. I will let some Jewish scholars speak, and they certainly understand their own language and customs.

Maimonides was born A. D. 1131, at Cordova, and died in 1204. He is called the Eagle of the Doctors and the Lamp of Israel. He was profoundly versed in the languages and in all the learning of the age, and became the physician of the Sultan of Egypt. He says: "Every person must dip his whole body . . . and wheresoever in the law washing of the body or garments is mentioned, it means nothing else than the whole body. For if any wash himself all over, except the tip of his little finger, he is still in his uncleanness. And if any have much hair, he must wash all the hairs of his head; for that also was received for the body. But if any should enter into the water with their clothes on, yet their washing holds good."

Leo of Modena, Rabbi of Venice, says: "He who desires to become a Jew, is first circumcised, and a few days afterwards is bathed in water in the presence of three Rabbis who have examined him." (De Rit. et Usis Judæorum, par. 1, c. 3.)

I addressed a letter to the two distinguished Rabbis mentioned below, and they very promptly responded. Rabbi Wise is widely known as a Jewish writer, scholar and preacher. He said:

CINCINNATI, OHIO, Jan. 3rd, 1883.

Dear Sir,—*Tabhal* signifies to submerge in a fluid or to dip a body into it, as is evident from numerous passages of Scripture. It is not *rahats*, to wash, nor *nazah*, to sprinkle.   Yours,

ISAAC M. WISE.

I here give the testimony of Rabbi B. Felsenthal, who is an orator of recognized ability, and has charge of one of the largest synagogues in this country:

WHAT THE SEPTUAGINT SAYS.

CHICAGO, Jan. 1st, 1883.

Dear Sir,—Your letter of Dec. 28th has been duly received. In answer I beg to state the following: It seems to me almost indisputable that the verb *tabhal* means to dip or to immerse. A comparison of all the passages in the Old Testament in which said verb is found—Gen. xxxvii: 31; Ex. xii: 22; Lev. iv: 6; also xiv: 6, 51; Num. xix: 18; Deut. xxxiii: 24; etc.—reveals the fact that in almost all of these passages the fluid is mentioned with *b* prefixed (*baddam*), into which the object of the act is to be *tabhal*; when sprinkling or squirting is meant, the verb *zaraq*, followed by the preposition *al*, upon, is employed. (See f. i. Ex. xxiv: 6, 8; xxix: 16, 20; Lev. xvii: 6; i: 5, 11; iii: 2, 8, 13; etc.) But aside from grammatical considerations and from the application of the word *tabhal* in the Old Testament, there are historical facts which prove beyond any doubt that *tabhal*, with the Jews in the times contemporary with Jesus and the Apostles, meant to immerse. The cases in consequence of which Israelites could become levitically unclean were very numerous. Every one who had touched a corpse, f. i. every woman in her menstruation, etc., was unclean, and had to be cleansed by *tebilah*. By this Neo-Hebraic noun, derived from the biblical word *tabhal*, the Jews eighteen and nineteen hundred years ago, and in all subsequent ages, designated immersion; and the Mishna, the whole Talmudic literature, is full of pharisaic details concerning the *tebilah*, setting forth the minimum size of the bathing vessels or of the natural basins, the volume of the water required, the nature of the water to be used in the act of purification. Historical allusions to *tebilah* which had actually taken place are also numerous; and a whole book might be filled if every thing that has been written by Jews concerning this matter, in the earliest Christian centuries, would be collected, and sifted and systematized, and commented upon. But this would be a work requiring long researches, and, consequently, several months' time.

The levitical laws concerning levitical purifications have become dead letters since the destruction of the temple in the year 70 A. D. Only in one instance are they still applied in the present day—by the very strict among the so-called orthodox Jews. Women, after the period of their menstruation is over, take a bath of purification. In the common parlance of the Jews of to-day it is called by the traditional name of *tebilah*, and for the act the verb *tabhal* is used; and this *tebilah* is always an immersion. If there are any Jews in your neighborhood, who are in the least acquainted with the usage of their people, they will corroborate you in this statement.

I have attempted, dear sir, to answer your question as fully as can be done in a letter, and in the short time to me for this answer. I shall be very glad if it gives you some satisfaction.

With the best regards,

Yours truly, B. FELSENTHAL.

I also addressed a letter to Prof. Franz Delitzsch, who was probably the most learned Oriental scholar in the world, and Professor in the renowned University of Leipzig, Germany. He was also an author of much celebrity in Old Testament exegesis, and I consider his admission as one of the most valuable made to our faith in our century. I put this question to him: "What is the literal meaning of the verb *tabhal?*" and he wrote this reply immediately under the question: "It signifies to *immerse*, the same as *baptizein.*"

I will close with a statement in Witsius' Works, London 1785, vol. 3, p. 364. He says of the Jewish baptisms: "The entire body was to be plunged at once: for if but the tip of the finger was undipt, and such a person was accounted to remain still in his uncleanness."

CHAPTER VI.

THE BAPTISM OF JOHN.

THIS baptism is graphically described by the Evangelist Mark: "John did baptize in the wilderness, and preach the baptism of repentance for the remission of sins. And there went out unto him all the land of Judea, and they of Jerusalem, and were all baptized of him in the river of Jordan, confessing their sins." (Comp. Math. iii: 5, 6.)

If we were to leave out of the question the meaning of the word *baptizo,* which I have demonstrated means to dip, the circumstances of this narrative would beyond all doubt point to immersion. John was baptizing *"in the river of Jordan."* He was not baptizing *at* the river but *in* the river. If the act John was performing was sprinkling or pouring, it will make good sense to substitute those words for baptize. Let us try it: "And were all sprinkled of him in the river Jordan." "Were all poured of him in the river Jordan." That is nonsense. The people were neither poured nor sprinkled into the river. Let us try once more: "And were all dipped of him in the river

Jordan." That reading is perfectly correct, and is the very thing the Evangelist was saying.

The most competent authorities fully admit that the baptism of John was an immersion in water. Hear them:—

Dr. Isaac Wise, the learned Jewish Rabbi of Cincinnati, in answer to a pamphlet of Mr. Heaton, says in the *American Israelite:* "Mr. Heaton confounds baptism with the sprinkling of the ashes of the red heifer, diluted in water, when the person or thing which had come in contact with a dead body. . . . . Any child, however, can see that there is also a sanitary clause involved in this law. There is no passage on record that John the Baptist thought of this case. The very fact that he went to the Jordan suggests that the case of Naaman with his leprosy, and the command of the prophet Elisha, was in the mind of the Baptist; and Naaman undoubtedly submerged his body seven times in the Jordan. If Mr. Heaton, instead of quibbling on words and consulting dictionaries, would have inquired after facts and would have looked up the matter in the Mishna, and other Jewish authors, he would have discovered that the Jews had no idea of sprinkling—they knew the bath and submersion. Consequently John the Baptist submerged his converts in the

Jordan. . . . . We know exactly what John did at the Jordan, and all the dictionaries cannot change the fact."

This is unprejudiced testimony.

The scholarly Meyer says, Com. Math. p. 77: "To this, however, the immersion of *the whole* of the baptized person, as the *metanoia*, was to purify the whole man, corresponded with profound significance, and to this the specially Christian view of the symbolical immersion and emersion afterwards connected itself by an ethical necessity."

Adam Clarke, the Methodist Commentator, at the end of his dissertation of Mark's Gospel, says: "The baptism of John was by plunging the body after this same manner as the washing of unclean persons was."

Dr. Bennett says, and his book is an authority in the Methodist Church and has the endorsement of Bishop Hurst: "The customary mode was used by the apostles in the baptism of the first converts. They were familiar with the baptism of John's disciples and of the Jewish proselytes. This was ordinarily by dipping or immersion. This is indicated not only by the general signification of the words used in describing the rite, but the earliest testimony of the documents which have been preserved gives preference." (Arch. p. 396.)

Geikie, an Episcopalian, in his popular Life of Christ, p. 276, says: "It was, hence, impossible to see a convert go down into a stream, travel-worn, and soiled with dust, and, after disappearing for a moment, emerge pure and fresh, without feeling that the symbol suited and interpreted a strong craving of the human heart. It was no formal rite with John. . . . . Bathing in Jordan had been a sacred symbol, at least, since the days of Naaman, but immersion by one like John, with strict and humiliating confession of sin, sacred vows of amendment, and hope of forgiveness, if they proved lasting, and all of this preparation for the Messiah, was something wholly new to Israel."

Dr. Dollinger, the great Catholic historian, says: "At first Christian baptism commonly took place in the Jordan; of course, as the Church spread more widely, also in private houses; like that of St. John, it was by immersion of the whole person, which is the only meaning of the New Testament word. A mere pouring or sprinkling was never thought of." (The First Age of Christ, and of the Church, p. 318.)

Archbishop Kenrick, Catholic, says: "As to the mode in which John baptized, many circumstances favor the opinion that it was by some kind of immersion." (Bap. p. 180.)

The statement in John iii: 23, is to the point,—"And John was also baptizing at Ænon near to Salim, because there was much water there; and they came, and were baptized."

The reason given for choosing Ænon is that there was sufficient water for baptismal purposes. He was baptizing in Ænon because there was much water there. It is objected that *polla hudata*, much water, may be translated "many waters." I might grant the "many streams" desired and yet there is sufficient water for baptizing. I read in Ps. xciii: 4, "The Lord on high is mightier than many waters, yea than the mighty waves of the sea." Ps. lxxvii: 19, "Thy way is in the sea, and thy paths in the great waters." The same phrase is applied to the rivers Tigris and Euphrates. The translation makes no difference as to the act of baptism. Stuart says any small stream would furnish water for immersion. (On Bap. p. 94.)

This is freely admitted by scholars.

Olshausen, Com. vol. 2, p. 365, says: "John was also baptizing in the neighborhood, because the water there, being deep, afforded convenience for immersion."

Lightfoot, Presbyterian, Works vol. 2, p. 121,

says: "That the baptism of John was by plunging the body seems to appear from those things related of him, namely, that he baptized in Jordan, that he baptized in Ænon, because there was much water there; and that Christ being baptized came up out of the water; to which that seems to be parallel, Acts viii: 38."

Calvin says: "From these words, John iii: 23, it may be inferred that baptism was administered by John and Christ, by plunging the whole body under water. Here we perceive how baptism was administered among the ancients; for they immersed the whole body in water."

Dr. Doddridge says, Epis. vol. 1, p. 158: "But nothing can be more evident than that *polla hudata*, many waters, signifies a large quantity of water, it being sometimes used for the Euphrates."

But does not the record read, Math. iii: 11, "I indeed baptize you with water," but "he shall baptize you with the Holy Ghost, and with fire"? Certainly, but you must remember this is the Episcopalian translation of King James. The original Greek has, they shall be baptized "in water," "in the Holy Ghost," and "in fire." For my part, I would rather take what God said than to trust any translation. The preposition "with" here, however, was not one of instrument. It represents the element into which the persons were to be dipped. They were to be baptized "with water," and not "with milk"; "with the Holy Spirit," and not "with honey"; "with fire," and not "with wine." Luther's translation recognizes this distinction, and translates this passage, "I indeed dip you with water." Meyer takes this position. He says, p. 81: "It is, agreeably to the connection of *baptizo*, not to be taken in an instrumental, but as in the meaning of the *element* in which baptism takes place."

The literal meaning of the passage is *in* water and not *with* water. It is so translated by Dr. Bennett, Arch. p. 389: "So that while the baptism of John was complete in water, *en hudati*, the baptism instituted by Christ was not only in water, but in the Holy Spirit and in fire, *pneumati hagio kai puri.*"

Dr. George Campbell, and Robinson in his Greek Lexicon, translate it: "In the Holy Ghost and in fire." Dr. George Campbell comments as follows: "In water, in the Holy Spirit, vulgate *in aqua, in spiritu sancto.* Thus also, the Syriac, and other ancient versions. All the modern translations from the Greek which I have seen, render the words as our common version does, except LeClerc. I am sorry to observe that the popish translators from the Vulgate have shown greater veneration for the style of that version than the generality of Protestant translators have shown for that of the original. For in this the Latin is not more explicit than the Greek, yet so inconsistent are the interpreters last mentioned, that none of these have scrupled to render *en to Jordana*, in the sixth verse, in *Jordan*, though nothing can be plainer than that, if there be any incongruity in the expression in water, this *in Jordan* must be equally incongruous. But they have seen that the preposition *in* could not be avoided there, without adopting a circumlocution, and saying, *with the water of Jordan*, which would have made their deviation from the text too glaring. The word *baptizein*, both in sacred authors and in classical, signifies *to dip, to plunge, to immerse*, and was rendered by Tertullian, the oldest of the Latin fathers, *tingere*, the term used for dyeing cloth, which was by immersion. It is always construed suitable to this meaning." (Four Gos., vol. 4, p. 23.)

Bishop Henry C. Potter, Episcopal Bishop of New York, says: "Now what was the drift of all of this, but at once to interpret and illustrate the meaning of his own baptizings. The outward act —that plunging in the Jordan—meant simply, get your bodies clean, and so it stood for that other call which rings through all of John the Baptist's preaching, "make your lives, so far as you can make them, white and clean." (Met. Pul., April, 1877.)

Prof. Plumptre, in Ellicott's Com., vol. 1, p. 12, says: "As heard and understood at the time, the baptism of the Holy Ghost would imply that the souls baptized would be plunged, as it were, in that creative and informing Spirit which was the source of hope and holiness and wisdom."

And in the parallel passage, Acts i : 5, vol. 1, p. 2, Prof. Plumptre also says: "Now they were told that their spirits were to be as fully baptized, *i. e.*, plunged into the power of the divine Spirit, as their bodies had been plunged into the waters of the Jordan."

Neander, Life of Christ, p. 53, says: "He it was who should baptize them with the Holy Ghost and with fire; that is to say, that as his, John's, followers were evidently immersed in the water, so the Messiah would immerse the souls of believers in the Holy Ghost imparted by himself; so that it should entirely penetrate their being, and form within them a principle of life."

And the Greek father Cyril of Jerusalem, who lived upon the very spot where the baptism of the Holy Spirit occurred, understood it as an immersion.

He remarks: "For the Lord saith, ye shall be immersed in the Holy Spirit not many days after this. Not impart the grace, but all-sufficing the power. For as he who sinks down into the waters and is immersed, is surrounded on all sides by the waters, so also they were completely immersed by the Spirit." (Instruc. VIII.)

CHAPTER VII.

THE BAPTISM OF JESUS.

THE baptism of Jesus is recorded in **Mark i: 9-11**: "And it came to pass in those days, that Jesus came from Nazareth of Galilee, and was baptized of John in Jordan. And straightway coming up out of the water, he saw the heavens opened, and the spirit like a dove descending upon him; and there came a voice from heaven, saying, Thou art my beloved Son, in whom I am well pleased."

This passage says in the original that he was baptized into the Jordan, and you can not pour or sprinkle a man into a river, and to say that Jesus was baptized with or at a river is a philological absurdity. There is not a man with ordinary intelligence, having no purpose to serve, and without prejudice, who could understand from this narrative any thing else than that Jesus was immersed into the Jordan.

So plainly does this scripture teach immersion, that the advocates of sprinkling have moved heaven and earth to turn aside this testimony, and have sought means to explain that it has no bearing upon our duty.

I will point out a few of these subterfuges:

1. "It is objected that the baptism of John was not Christian baptism." Our Pedobaptist brethren borrow this objection from the Catholics. Archbishop Kenrick says: "We are not authorized by any expression of the sacred writers, to consider the baptism of John as a rite of divine institution." (Bap. p. 16.) But the Scriptures expressly say, that "John was sent from God;" and that his baptism was not "from men," but from "God." Every element of Christian baptism was present in the act required by John. There was "repentance," Mark i: 4; "faith," Acts xix: 4; "confession," Mark i: 5, and then baptism. All the persons of the Trinity witnessed the baptism of Jesus and took part in it. The Father spoke his approval, the Holy Spirit came as a dove and sat upon him, while the Son was baptized. If Jesus received the baptism of John without a question, why should you seek to throw doubt upon it?

2. "It was to initiate Jesus into the priesthood." The misfortune of this theory is that it is not found in the Scriptures. This assertion is a pure gratuity. Jesus Christ never was a Jewish priest, nor did he ever lay claim to any such office. He was not of the priestly tribe of Levi: he be-

longed to the kingly tribe of Judah. As a Jew, it would have been criminal, instead of praiseworthy, for our Lord to have appropriated to himself any of the ceremonies belonging solely to the tribe of Levi. This charge was never brought against Jesus, as it certainly would have been, had there been any foundation for it in pretense or fact. Jesus laid no claim to the Jewish priesthood. He was a high-priest, but it was after the order of Melchisedec and not of Aaron. He did not have "to be initiated into the priesthood at the age of thirty years;" but he was a priest "forever after the order of Melchisedec;" and he abideth "a priest continually." (Heb. vii : 17.) The Scriptures are absolutely silent on the statement that Jesus was a Jewish priest.

3. But it is objected that John's baptism was one of purification. If I should grant that proposition, baptism could still be a dipping in water. I ask which would more likely represent purification, a few drops of water on the head, or a complete baptism in water? But what will you do with this theory in the baptism of Jesus? He needed no purification. He was without sin, and neither was guile found in his mouth. He was pure and holy and separate from sinners. This will not bear investigation for a moment.

Hear what the learned Neander says: "The idea that Christ was baptized with a view of purification is absolutely untenable, no matter how the notion of purification may be modified." (Life of Christ, p. 64.)

The best way to do is to take this passage as it reads. Jesus was immersed into the river of Jordan. So certain is this that Pedobaptist scholars have freely acknowledged it. I shall quote only a few.

Last year Dr. Maclaren, of England, in his exposition of the "Sunday School Lessons," in the *Sunday School Times*, said that Jesus was immersed. At once a number of gentlemen wrote a protest to Dr. Trumbull, editor of the *Times*. In an editorial, Aug. 6th, 1889, he replied: "Most Christian scholars of every denomination are agreed in finding the primitive meaning of the word baptize to be 'to dip,' or 'to immerse.' The sweep of scholarship in and out of the Baptist church is in favor of immersion as a principle meaning of the word baptize. A very large portion of the scholars of the world agree with Dr. Maclaren that immersion was the mode of John's baptism."

Dr. Hibbard, the standard Methodist writer on baptism, says: "Jesus was baptized . . . into the Jordan. In the latter case we have no doubt of an outward baptism, and the words *eis ton Jordanan*, into the Jordan, beyond all contradiction, affix to the verb baptize its literal signification." (Bapt. P. 2, p. 132.)

Bishop Jeremy Taylor, Episcopalian, says: "Straightway Jesus went up out of the water (saith the Gospel); he came up, therefore he went down. Behold an immersion, not an aspersion. And the ancient churches, followed this of the Gospel, did not, in their baptisms, sprinkle water with their hands, but immerged the catechumen or infant. . . . . All which are a perfect conviction, that the custom of the ancient churches was not sprinkling, but immersion, in pursuance of the meaning of the word in the commandment, and the example of our blessed Saviour." (Works, vol. 14, p. 62.)

So generally is it understood that Jesus was immersed in the Jordan, that thousands of people are immersed, or immerse themselves, at the reputed place of the baptism of Jesus. In 1890 Dr. Talmage, a Presbyterian preacher, baptized a man at this place. Dean Stanley describes a scene that takes place every year in the Jordan. "Of all the practices," says Stanley, "superstitions, if we choose so to call them, of the Oriental churches in Palestine, none is more innocent or natural than the ceremony repeated year by year at the Greek Easter—the bathing of the pilgrims in the Jordan. It has often been witnessed by European travellers. I venture to describe it from my own recollections, for the sake of the general illustration which it furnishes of the present forms of Oriental Christianity, and also as presenting the nearest likeness that can now be seen in the same general scenery to the multitudinous baptisms of John. Once a year—on the Monday in Passion-week— the desolation of the plain of Jericho is broken by the descent from the Judean hills of five, six, or eight thousand pilgrims. . . . They dismount, and set to work to perform their bath; most on the open space, some further up amongst the thickets; some plunging in naked, most, however, with white dresses, which they bring with them, and which, having been so used, are kept for their winding sheets. Most of the bathers keep within the shelter of the bank, where the water is about four feet deep, though with a bottom of very deep mud. . . . A primitive domestic character pervades in a singular form the whole transaction. The families which have come on their single mule or camel, now bathe together, with the utmost gravity; the father receiving from the mother the infant, which has been brought to receive the one immersion which will suffice for the rest of his life, and thus, by a curious economy of resources, save it from the expense and danger of a future pilgrimage in after years. In about two hours the shores are cleared; with the same quiet they remount their camels and horses; and before the noonday heat has set in, are again encamped on the upper plain of Jericho." (Sinai and Pal. p. 386.)

There remains but one question. If, as I have shown, Jesus was immersed, is it not your duty to be baptized also; and if Jesus went down into the water, is it not your duty to do the same? You have no right to set up your opinion against the example of the Son of God. "Where he leads I will follow," is an excellent rule to obey.

CHAPTER VIII.

THE BAPTISM MENTIONED IN MARK vii: 1-4.

THIS scripture reads: "There came together unto him the Pharisees, and certain of the scribes, which came from Jerusalem. And when they saw some of the disciples eat bread with defiled, that is to say, with unwashed hands, they found fault. For the Pharisees, and all of the Jews, except they wash their hands oft, eat not, holding the tradition of the elders. And when they come from the market, except they wash, they eat not. And many other things there be, which they have received to hold, as the washing of cups, and pots, brazen vessels, and of tables."

There are three things here that demand notice:

1. The Pharisees were accustomed to wash their hands (*niptontai*) before they eat. They would take a basin of water, plunge their hands into it and rub them clean. Robinson says in his Greek lexicon of this practice, "unless they wash their hands (rubbing them) with the fist, *i. e.*, not merely dipping the fingers or hands in water as a *sign* of ablution, but rubbing the hands together as a ball or fist, in the usual Oriental manner when water is

poured over them (2 K., iii: 1), see in *nipto*, hence *ad sensum*, sedulously, diligently." Perhaps Kitto more accurately describes the act (Cy. vol. 1, p. 18): "The hands were plunged in water. It was this last, namely the ceremonial ablution, which the **Pharisees** judged to be necessary. When therefore some of that sect remarked that our Lord's diciples ate 'with unwashed hands,' it is not to be understood literally, that they did not at all wash their hands, but that they did not plunge them ceremonially according to their own practice."

This word, however, never refers to the ordinance of baptism.

2. When the Pharisees came from the market they baptized themselves before they ate. Loud and deep has been the denial that *baptizo* here means to dip. But it cannot be asserted that such an immersion "is either an impossible or an improbable one; for surely the Jews could have immersed themselves after coming from the market; and that they did practice ablution by immersion, in many cases besides those precribed by the law of Moses, is matter of historical proof. Besides, the consistency and harmony of the passage requires that *baptizo* have a more extensive meaning than *nipto*. To read it, "The Pharisees and all the Jews, except they wash their hands, eat not; and when

they come from the market, except they wash they eat not," makes an unmeaning tautology. It is stated in the first place, that they on all occasions wash their hands previous to eating; what, then, does it add to the sense, to say, that when they come from the market, they do not eat without washing? The evangelist evidently intends to be understood, that all the Jews, on all occasions, wash their hands before eating; and that when they have been to the forum, or place of public concourse, they practice a more extensive purification. *Baptizo*, then, may not only have its usual signification here, but that meaning is absolutely required by the scope and harmony of the passage."

It is also a fact that *rantizontai*, sprinkling, is in the text of many Greek editions of the New Testament. Westcott and Hort has that reading, and the Revised version adds, "Some ancient authorities read sprinkle themselves." Such a reading, of course, would relieve immersionists of any supposed difficulty in regard to this text.

I am, however, content to let the common reading remain. Thayer, Stephanus, and the Greek lexicons generally say that the Pharisees immersed or bathed themselves; while Dr. George Campbell, Noyes, and other scholars render the word by immersion or dip. I shall let the scholars testify.

Dr. H. Holtzmann, of Strasburg University, writes me, April 4th, 1890, that "*baptizo* means to dip, and that washing for ablution could possibly be the meaning in Mark vii : 1–4; but even there it is wrong, since the passage refers to ablution by dipping under before meal-time. Moreover, *rantizontai*, and not *baptizontai*, is the proper reading."

Dr. George Campbell, Presbyterian, says: "The first is *niptontai*, properly translated to wash; the second is *baptizontai*, which limits its meaning to a particular kind of washing; for *baptizo* means to plunge, to dip." (Four Gos. vol. 4, p. 205.)

Olshausen, Lutheran, says: "The term *baptizesthai* is different from *niptesthai;* the former is the dipping and rinsing, or cleansing of food that has been purchased, to free it from impurities of any kind; *niptesthai* includes also the act of rubbing off." (Com. vol. 1, p. 527.)

Prof. Plumptre, in Ellicott's Com. vol. 1, p. 207, says: "The Greek verb differs from that of the previous verse, and implies the washing or immersion (the verb is that from which our word 'baptize' comes to us) of the whole body, as the former does of part. The idea on which the practice rested was not one of cleanliness or health, but of arrogant exclusiveness, fastening on the thought of ceremonial purity. They might have come, in the crowd of the market, into passing contact with a **Gentile,** and his touch was as defiling as a corpse. So, too, the washing of cups and the like was because they might have been touched by a heathen, and therefore impure lips."

The great exegete, Meyer, says: "In this case *ean ma baptisontai* is not to be understood of washing the hands, but of immersion, which the word in classic Greek and in the New Testament denotes; *i. e.* in this case, according to the context, to take a bath. So, also, Lu. ix: 38; Comp. Eccl. xxx: 25; Judith xii: 7. Having come from market, where they may have contracted pollution through contact with the crowd, they eat not without having first bathed. The statement proceeds by way of climax: Before eating they observe the washing of hands always, but the bathing when they come from market and wish to eat." (Com. Mark vii: 4.)

3. The immersion of pots, brazen vessels and tables. The main objection offered to this is that it is not probable that "tables" were immersed. Such authorities as Tischendorf, and Westcott and Hort, entirely omit tables from the text; but to be absolutely fair, granting that it is a genuine reading, we are at no loss. It certainly is not impossible to immerse an Oriental table. Indeed noth-

ing would be easier. "The table in the East," says Jahn, "is a piece of round leather, spread upon the floor, upon which is placed a sort of stool. This supports nothing but a platter."

But it is objected that this does not mean table, but a "couch or bed." But that does not help the case of our opponents. The Eastern bed is quite as movable as the table. "The manner of sleeping in warm Eastern climates," says Kitto, "is necessarily very different from that which is followed in our colder regions. The present usages appear to be the same as those of the ancient Jews, and sufficiently explain the passages of Scripture which bear on that subject. Beds of feathers are altogether unknown, and the Orientals generally lie exceedingly hard. Poor people have no certain home, and when on a journey, or employed at a distance from their dwelling, sleep on mats or wrapped in their outer garment, which, from its importance in this respect, was forbidden to be retained in pledge over night. Under peculiar circumstances a stone covered with some folded cloth or piece of dress is often used for a pillow. The more wealthy classes sleep on mattresses stuffed with wool or cotton, which often are no other than a quilt thickly padded, and are used either singly, or one or more placed upon each other." (Cy. vol. 1, p. 311.)

The law of Moses positively required many things to be put in water. If a dead thing fall upon a person or thing, it must be put into water. (Lev. xi: 32.) And other things were to go through "the water." (Num. xxxi: 23.) Those laws that were already stringent were greatly added to by the Pharisees. Maimonides, a Jewish commentator, states that it was a traditional custom of the Jews to immerse all vessels for eating, drinking, and cooking, whether had of a Gentile or an Israelite. "Vessels," he says, "bought of Gentiles for the use of a feast, whether molten or glass vessels, they immerse in the waters of the laver, and after that they may eat and drink in them; and such as they used for cold things, as cups, pots, and jugs, they washed them and immersed them, and they are free for use; and such as they use for hot things, as cauldrons and kettles, or brazen vessels, they heat them with hot water, and scour them and immerse them, and they are fit to be used; and things which they use at the fire, as spits and gridirons, they heat them in the fire, and immerse them, and they may be lawfully made use of. This is the immersion with which they immerse vessels for a feast, bought of Gentiles." (Maacolot. c. 17, sec. 3, 5, 6.) Again the same author says: "Vessels, they say, that are furnished in purity, that is, by Jews, even though the disciple of a wise man makes them, care is to be taken about them; lo! these ought to be immersed." "A bed that is wholly defiled if one immerses it part by part." (Hilch. Abot. Hatum. c. 12, sec. 6; Hilch. Mikvaot, c. 1, sec. 2.)

There is nothing in this passage that will make an immersionist change his opinion.

CHAPTER IX.

THE BAPTISM OF THE THREE THOUSAND.

IN the second chapter of the Acts of the Apostles, it is said that after Peter's sermon, "the same day there were added about three thousand souls" to the disciples. This statement has been regarded by Pedobaptists in general as a very serious objection to the act of baptism by immersion. Indeed it is their strong fort; it is the last rallying place. To me it is a very weak and childish argument. As it appears to have such great force, I shall notice it at length.

Take, for example, the standard Methodist writer, Dr. T. O. Summers. In his Treatise, p. 86, under his "proofs of affusion," he says: "It was impossible for the twelve apostles to immerse such a multitude in some six or eight hours." If Dr. Summers had been as good in arithmetic as he was in surmising "proofs for affusion," this assertion would have never been made. You will notice that according to this statement the apostles would have baptized less than thirty-one persons each in an hour, and nothing would be easier for a Baptist preacher than that. In this brief sentence there are some very violent suppositions. I shall point them out separately.

1. He presumes that the entire three thousand were baptized in one day. The Scripture only says they "were added." There is no record that they were all baptized upon one day; but so far as the Bible states, they may have been baptized upon the following days. You say that this is a Baptist dodge. Not a bit of it. This position is endorsed by the strongest scholars. I have before me the declaration of Dr. Dollinger, who was the greatest Catholic writer of this century. He was the Professor of Church History in the University of Bonn, and recently passed to rest full of honors. He is surely a disinterested witness. He says in his History of the Church, vol. 1, p. 319: "It is not said that the three thousand converts of Pentecost were all baptized the same day, but only "on that day were added three thousand souls" (Acts ii: 41); *i. e.* their conversion and belief took place on that day; they were baptized on the following days, of course, gradually, and accordingly the fact of their baptism is mentioned without any time being assigned."

Prof. C. W. Bennett, D.D., says: "No evidence, however, is furnished by the record that Peter himself baptized three thousand believers on the day of Pentecost. This may have been done by different apostles at different places, by different modes, during the entire day, or subsequent days." (Arch. p. 396.)

2. It is a common matter of history that as many as three thousand persons have often been baptized in one day. I shall mention time, place, and give the authority upon which I make this declaration.

The first instance is that of Chrysostom, baptizing three thousand in Constantinople, on the 16th of April, A. D. 404. Perthes, in his Life of St. Chrysostom, p. 185, says: "On Easter eve, the 16th of April, the Church of Chrysostom and the friendly clergy met together, as was the custom, to spend the night in vigils and to greet the rays of the Easter morning. With them were assembled three thousand young Christians who were to receive baptism." Cave, in his Lives of the Fathers, London 1716, p. 661, gives an account of the baptism of this three thousand, and then relates a most horrid story of how the Church was desecrated by the soldiers and the entire city scattered. Chrysostom himself tells us how the act of baptism was performed. "For we sink our heads in the water," says he, "as if in some grave, the old man is buried; and the whole man, having sunk entirely down, is concealed. Then, we emerge him, the new man rises again. For as it is easy for us to be immersed and to emerge, so it is easy for God to bury the old man and to bring to light the new. This is done three times." (Patrol. Lat. Minge, vol. 59, p. 151.) If Chrysostom could immerse three thousand converts in one night when the soldiers threatened his life and drove him from his church, it would seem an easy thing for Peter to immerse a like number when he had favor with all the people, as he did have on the day of Pentecost.

The second instance is that of St. Patrick, of Ireland. During his life he is said to have immersed one hundred and twenty thousand people. Dr. Todd, an Episcopalian, Professor of Hebrew in Trinity College, Dublin, and a ripe Irish scholar, says in his life of Patrick, p. 442: "Patrick entered into the king's palace, and he said to Hercus, (after some conversation) Wilt thou receive the baptism of the Lord, which I have with me? He answered, I will receive it; and they came to the fountain Loigles, and when he had opened his book and had baptized the man Hercus, he heard men behind his back mocking him one to another about the matter, for they knew not what he had done. And he baptized many thousand on that day." On p. 449, Dr. Todd says: "He penetrated the hearts of all and led them to embrace cordially the Christian faith and doctrine. The seven sons of Amalgaidh, with the king himself and twelve thousand men were baptized. They were baptized in a well (fountain) called Tobur-en-adare." Rev. J. O'Farrell, in his popular Life of St. Patrick, p. 157, says: "After descending from the mountain, invigorated for the sacred duties of the ministry, St. Patrick came to the district of Corcothemne—not far distant, it would seem—and to the fountain of Sinn, where he baptized many thousands." In these lives of St. Patrick there are repeated mention of fountain baptisms which of necessity were by immersion. Indeed, so late as the twelfth century, Gilbert, Bishop of Limerick, in Ireland, in his little book, The Constitution of the Church, says of the priest: "It is his duty to administer baptism, to dip believers who have been exorcised and who have confessed the Holy Trinity, with three immersions in the sacred font." (Patrol. Lat. vol. 159, p. 1000.) Here are twelve thousand men immersed in one day, and several thousands on other days.

The third instance which I present is that of Clovis, king of France. He was baptized in

Rheims by Remingius, on Christmas day, A. D. 496. Thanks to that magnificent collection of the Christian Fathers—*Patrologia Latinæ*—I have all the original documents before me. Hincmar, the successor of Remingius, says, that not only was the king baptized, but "from his army three thousand men were baptized, without counting women and children." (Patrol. Lat. vol. 125, pp. 1159, 1162.) Gregory of Tours, who wrote a valuable history of France, in 574, says, they were baptized "in a fresh fountain," and gives the details of the immersion. Avitus, Bishop of Vienna, was so pleased that he wrote the king a letter in which he says: "That it might appear in due order that you were born again out of the water for salvation on that day on which the world received the Lord of Heaven, born for its redemption." (Patrol. Lat., vol. 71, p. 1154.) Alcuin also says of his baptism: " He (Remingius) led the eager king to the fountain of life, and when he came he washed him in the fountain of eternal salvation. So the king was baptized with his nobles and people, who rejoiced to receive the sacrament of the healing bath, divine grace having been previously given them." (Patrol. Lat., vol. 101, p. 670.) If there can be any sort of doubt as to what Alcuin meant by washing him in a fountain, he says elsewhere that baptism was by "trine immersion." (Patrol. Lat., vol. 100, p. 291.) The testimony of Hincmar will set the matter at rest. He says: "After confessing the orthodox faith in answer to questions put by the holy pontiff, according to ecclesiastical custom he was baptized by trine immersion in the name of the holy and undivided Trinity, Father, Son, and Holy Spirit." (Patrol. Lat., vol. 125, p. 1162.) This immersion can not be called in question.

The fourth instance I present is that of Augustine. He baptized 10,000 men, not counting women and children, in the Swale, in one day. In Fabyan's Chronicles, London 1811, p. 96, I read: "He had in one day christened ten thousands of Saxons or Angles in the west river, which is called Swale, beside York." Henry, in his History of England, confirms this statement. (Vol. 3., p. 192.) I have before me a letter of Pope Gregory to Eulogius, Patriarch of Alexandria, informing him of this great victory. "More than ten thousand English," says he, "they tell us, were baptized by the same brother, our fellow bishop, which I communicate to you to announce to the people of Alexandria, and that you may do something in prayer for the dwellers at the ends of the earth." (Patrol. Lat., vol. 77, p. 951.) Gregory evidently understood this to mean an immersion, for he said:

"We baptize by trine immersion." (Patrol. Lat., vol. 77, p. 498. Gocelyn, in his Life of Augustine, has this to say: "He secured on all sides large numbers for Christ, so that on the birth-day of the Lord, celebrated by the melodious anthems of all heaven, more than ten thousand of the English were born again in the laver of holy baptism, with an infinite number of women and children, in a river which the English call Sirarios, the Swale, as if at one birth of the church from the womb. These persons, at the command of the divine teacher, as if he were an angel from heaven, calling upon them, all entered the dangerous depths of the river, two and two together, as if it had been a solid plain; and in true faith, confessing the exalted Trinity, they were baptized one by the other in turns, the apostolic leader blessing the water. . . . So great a prodigy from heaven born out of the deep whirlpool." (Patrol. Lat., vol. 80, p. 79.) Here are more than three times the number of Pentecost, not counting women and children.

I would also call attention to the baptism of Paulinus of ten thousand English in the river Swale. I quote from the learned Camden, in his Britannia, London 1806, vol. 3, p. 257, the Swale "was accounted sacred by the ancient Saxons, above

BAPTISM OF THE THREE THOUSAND.

the ten thousand persons, besides women and children, having received baptism in it, in one day from Paulinus, Archbishop of York, on the first conversion of the Saxons to Christianity."

If there still lingers a doubt as to these river baptisms of Augustine and Paulinus, I would refer you to the Roman Catholic historian of the early English Church, John Lingard, D.D., vol. 1, p. 291: "The regular manner of administering baptism was by immersion."

The sixth instance took place in Germany. St. Boniface is said to have immersed 100,000 converts during his life. Othelon, in his Life of Boniface, gives an account of a large number who were baptized at one time by him. "Then also he entered," says he, "other parts of Germany that he might preach. He went to the Hessians located on the confines of the Saxons, whom in like manner, he converted in large numbers from paganism, and he washed many thousands of men in the sacrament of baptism." (St. Boniface Mogunt Arch. vita c. 12 srpt., Eccl. viii. sæc. Migne.) Pope Zacharias in a letter to Boniface fully explains what is meant by this "washing." "Whosoever has been washed," says the Pope, "without the invocation of the Trinity, has not the sacrament of regeneration (baptism), as it is assuredly true that if any one has been immersed in the baptismal fountain without the invocation of the Trinity, he has not been made perfect until he shall have been baptized in the name of the Father, and of the Son, and of the Holy Spirit. . . . Whosoever is immersed, the Trinity being invoked in Gospel language after the rule laid down by the Lord, in the name of the Father, and of the Son, and of the Holy Ghost, has that sacrament without doubt. . . . But about those who immerse in the fountain of baptism without the invocation of the Trinity, it is known to thy fraternity that the series of sacred rules contain something which we advise you to hold tenaciously." (Zach. Pop., pp. 943, 994, Migne.)

The seventh instance is found in Pomerania. Bishop Otto, 1124, preached on a missionary tour in that country. An account of this is given in Neander's Church History, vol. 4, p. 8. "Seven days," says the historian, "were spent by the bishop in giving instruction; three days were appointed for spiritual and bodily preparation to receive the ordinance of baptism. They held a fast and bathed themselves, that they might with cleanliness and decency submit to the holy transaction. Large vessels filled with water were sunk into the ground and surrounded with curtains. Behind these baptism was administered, in the form customary at that period, by immersion. During the twenty days residence in that town, some thousands were baptized; and the persons baptized were instructed on the matters contained in the confession of faith and respecting the most important acts of worship."

The eighth example is the introduction of Christianity into Russia. The Russian ruler, Vladimir, accepted Christ, and after his baptism he commanded all the people of Kieff to be baptized. Accordingly on a set day thousands of the people of this city were immersed in the river. Dean Stanley gives the following account of this transaction: Vladimir "was baptized accordingly at Cherson, and then issued orders for a great baptism of his people at Kieff. . . . The whole people of Kieff were immersed in the same river, some sitting on the banks, some plunged in, others swimming, whilst the priest read the prayers. It was a sight, says Nestor, wonderfully curious and beautiful to see; and when the whole people were baptized, each one returned to his own house." The spot was consecrated by the first Christian church, and Kieff, which had already, which we have seen from old traditions, been the Glastonbury, became henceforward the Canterbury of the Russian Empire." (East. Ch., p. 291.)

The last instance records the wonderful success of one of our devoted missionaries. In the Madras Confederacy, in 1878, Bro. J. E. Clough, with five assistants, baptized in six hours, two baptizing at a time, 2,222 converts. On December 28th, 1890, 1,671 more were baptized. As these baptisms were performed by Baptist preachers I shall scarcely be expected to offer proof that the act was by immersion.

The truth is that all the great baptisms of the world have been by immersion.

Here are nine examples where thousands were baptized by immersion in one day. These facts will not only answer any quibble that may be offered upon the "baptism of the three thousand," but demonstrates that immersion was possible and probable.

CHAPTER X.

THE BAPTISM OF THE ETHIOPIAN EUNUCH.

ACTS viii: 38, 39: "They went down both *into* the water, both Philip and the eunuch, and he baptized him. And when they came up *out of the water* the Spirit of the Lord caught away Philip."

This example is overwhelmingly in favor of immersion. The force of the preposition in this narrative can not be overstated. They went down into the water, and came up out of the water. There is not a child ten years old that does not know what is meant here, and exactly what took place. It takes a wise man to explain away this passage; and when he gets through explaining, immersion is there still.

They went into the water, and came up out of the water. It does not say they went to the pool's brink, but they went into the water, and they came out of the water. I have an idea that when God says they went into the water, that is exactly what happened. I shall illustrate by rather an amusing incident: There was in this State an old Baptist preacher full of wit. He heard a man preach, who was not a Baptist, and he took great pains to show that "into" in this scripture meant near by, at, in the neighborhood of. The next day the old man saw this preacher walking in front of a saloon. He said nothing, but walked up the street till he met one of his prominent members, and told him he saw his preacher down the street in a saloon. The preacher immediately denied this statement as a foul slander, and tried to make the old man take it back. "I was not in the saloon," said he; "I only passed by it." "But," said the old man, "'into,' yesterday, meant near by, in the neighborhood of, and I thought it meant the same thing to-day. It means one thing in a sermon, and another thing in every-day life." No, sir; they both went down into the water, and Philip immersed the eunuch.

The best Pedobaptist authorities agree with us fully on this position.

John Calvin, Presbyterian, says: "Here we perceive how baptism was administered among the ancients, for they immersed the whole body in water."

Dr. Doddridge says: "It would be very irrational to suppose that they went down to the water merely that Philip might take up a *little water in his hand* to pour on the eunuch. A person of his dignity had, no doubt, many vessels in his baggage on such a journey through so desert a country—a precaution absolutely necessary for *travelers* in those parts, and never omitted by them." (Vol. 3, p. 119.)

Bishop Ellicott in his Commentary says: "The Greek preposition might mean simply '*unto*' the water, but the universality of immersion in the practice of the early church supports the English version. The eunuch would lay aside his garments, descend chest deep into the water, and be plunged under it 'in the name of the Lord Jesus'—the only formula recognized in the Acts." (Com. vol. 2, p. 54.)

Homersham Cox in his recent researches declares: "This (immersion) was clearly the mode of baptizing the Ethiopian eunuch: 'They both went down into the water, both Philip and the eunuch, and he baptized him.'" (The First Cen. of Christ. p. 277.)

The scholars teach that this passage means immersion.

But this objection is urged. Philip read to the eunuch the fifty-third chapter of Isaiah, and in the fifteenth verse of the preceding chapter occurs the phrase, "so shall he sprinkle many nations." It is taken for granted that this "sprinkling" means baptism. There is no mention made of water and none of baptism in this scripture. "So" in this verse must refer to "as" in verse 14 to complete the antithesis. The one is commensurate with the other. In verse 14 he is telling how Jesus shall astonish the nations by his great sufferings; and this verse must correspond with the other. If this is the case, baptism is not the question discussed, but the sufferings of the Son of God. The word sprinkle then would refer to the expiation Christ has made for our sins. This is often so expressed in the Scriptures, as in Heb. x: 22: "Let us draw near with a true heart in full assurance of faith, having *our hearts sprinkled from an evil conscience,* and our bodies washed with pure water."

This passage can not refer to baptism because the word sprinkle is used. Sprinkle is never used for baptism in the Bible. *Baptizo,* and that alone, is the word that describes the ordinance of baptism. This all scholars admit. Furthermore, it says he shall sprinkle many nations. Baptism has nothing to do with nations; it is a personal matter; something that each man must perform for himself. The commission is, "He that believeth and is baptized shall be saved." The New Testament always places it in this light, and in none other.

The best scholars say that the word *nazah*, here rendered to sprinkle, means to astonish. Gesenius defines *nazah*, "to leap, to spring, to exult, to leap for joy; when applied to liquids, to spirt, to spatter, to besprinkle." (Lex. p. 658.) But this passage does not refer to liquids; it refers to nations. But admitting that the word means to sprinkle, we have not one particle of proof that the passage has the most distant application to baptism.

George R. Noyes, Professor of Hebrew in Harvard University, in his New Translation of the Hebrew Prophets, 1833, renders Isaiah lii: 14, 15, thus:

> "As many were amazed at the sight of him,
> So disfigured and scarcely human was his visage,
> And his form so unlike that of man,
> So shall many nations exult on account of him,
> And kings shall shut their mouths before him;
> For what had never been told them shall they see,
> And what they never heard shall they perceive."

Dr. Barnes, the eminent Presbyterian scholar, after fully discussing the various meanings of the word, says: "It may be remarked that whichever of the above senses may be assigned, it furnishes no argument for the practice of sprinkling in baptism. It refers to the fact of his purifying or cleansing the nations, and not to the ordinance of Christian baptism; nor should it be used as an argument in reference to the mode in which that should be administered."

But this is not all. Two hundred and eighty-five years before Christ the Old Testament was translated into Greek. This was done by seventy-two learned men appointed for the purpose. Those rabbis understood the Hebrew perfectly well, and they translated this word *nazah* by the Greek word *thaumazo*, to astonish, a word which never means to sprinkle. To show how authoritative this translation is, it is only necessary to state that our Saviour and his apostles used it nearly altogether.

From whatever standpoint we look at this passage it can mean nothing but immersion.

CHAPTER XI.

PAUL'S BAPTISM.

PEDOBAPTISTS say more of Paul's baptism than of any other in the New Testament; yet, when rightly considered, it affords them no argument whatever. This Scripture reads as follows:—

"And why tarriest thou? arise, and be baptized, and wash away thy sins, calling on the name of the Lord." (Acts xxii: 16.)

I shall examine some points in this Scripture.

It must be remembered that this is the proof text of the Pedobaptists, and if I answer all objections, and show that this passage is not inconsistent with, and is even favorable to immersion, I have accomplished all that is necessary to my argument.

"Arise." They make great capital out of this word. "Paul," say they, "simply got up and was baptized where he stood." Does *anastas*, the Greek word for arise, mean a standing still? It does not. The man may or may not stand still. Liddell and Scott not only say it means to "arise," but to make "people arise to leave their homes."

And Thayer says, "those who leave a place to go elsewhere; hence, of those who prepare themselves for a journey." Robinson, "He arose and followed." According to the Lexicons Paul arose and went to another place and was baptized. May I suggest one of the "rivers of Damascus?" (2 Kings v: 12.)

Do the instances where *anastas* occur, imply a standing still after the person has arisen? Homer relates that Ulysses came in with a stag on his shoulders, threw it down and said to his companions, "arise and eat." Yet the stag had to be prepared and cooked before they ate, and parts of it were eaten in another place. This participle is used several times in the ninth chapter of the Acts, where the baptism of Paul is mentioned, and always with the idea of motion. Verse 11th: "arise, and go into the street that is called Straight;" v. 18th, "he arose and was baptized;" vs. 34th, "Eneas, Jesus Christ maketh thee whole; arise, and make thy bed." Acts x: 13, "Arise, Peter, slay and eat;" v. 20th, "arise thee, therefore, and get thee down." Every one of these examples shows that the persons did not stand still. I have not found a single example where *anastas* does not imply motion.

"Be Baptized." If there was no other word in

this entire sentence this would be sufficient to tell what was meant. As Connybeare and Howson say: "He was baptized, and the rivers of Damascus became more to him than all the waters of Judah." (Life and Epis. p. 89.) Or as Bishop Ellicott says in his Commentary: "The baptism would probably be administered in one or the other of the rivers which the history of Naaman had made famous, and so the waters of Abana and Pharpar, rivers of Damascus, were now sanctified no less than the Jordan for the "mystical washing away of sin." But Paul himself tells how he was baptized: "We are buried with him by baptism into death." (Rom. vi: 3.) The "we" includes himself along with the Romans. This is a clear case of immersion.

"Wash away thy sins." The word used for wash is *louo*, in the middle voice. There are words to express the washing of the several parts of the body; but *louo* means the washing or bathing of the entire body. In the active voice it means to wash, to bathe; and in the middle voice a washing by bathing. As a learned and candid writer has said that if the word baptize was doubtful, the use of *louo* would settle Paul's baptism. Here is what the Lexicons say. Dr. Robinson: *Louo* " signifies to wash the entire body, not merely a part of it, like *nipto*." Trench: "*Niptein* and *nipsasthai* almost always express the washing of a part of the body; while *louein*, which is not so much 'to wash' as 'to bathe,' and *lousthai*, or in common Greek *louesthai*, to 'bathe one's self,' imply always not the bathing of a part of the body, but of the whole." Liddell and Scott: "Wash the body, to wash one's self, to bathe." Thayer says, "*louo* refers to the whole of the body, *nipto* to a part."

Louo was plainly used in this signification among the Greeks. Homer represents a star just rising fresh from ocean's bath. He also says of some of the companions of Telemachus:—

"Thence to the bath, a beauteous pile, descend."

Jupiter gives direction to Apollo to cleanse the body of Sarpedon, and then bathe it in the river.

"'Phœbus, my son, delay not from beneath
Yon hill of weapons drawn, cleanse from his blood
Sarpedon's corse; then, bearing him remote,
Lave him in waters of the running stream."

In the Bible it is used: 1. As synonymous with baptize. (2 Kings v: 10, 14.) Elisha told Naaman to go and wash, and he went and dipped himself in the Jordan. 2. It is used for baptize in Heb. x: 22: "Having your bodies washed or bathed in pure water." Here the entire body is to be washed. This washing was, therefore, equal to an immersion. I can not refrain from referring to two poets who have spoken of the washing of our bodies as emblematic of the washing away of sin. Milton says:

> "Them who shall believe
> Baptized in the profluent stream, the sign
> Of washing them from the guilt of sin to life
> Pure, and in him prepared, if so befall,
> For death, like that which the Redeemer died."

Cowper said:

> "There is a fountain filled with blood,
> Drawn from Immanuel's veins,
> And sinners plunged beneath that flood
> Lose all their guilty stains."

I would therefore record it as my earnest conviction that this passage teaches immersion.

CHAPTER XII.

THE BAPTISM OF THE JAILER.

THE baptism of the jailer appears to give some of our Pedobaptist brethren a good deal of comfort. Thus Dr. Summers states the case from the Methodist standpoint: "The Philippian jailer too must have been baptized by affusion. His conversion took place in the prison—at midnight—and he and all his were baptized straightway. We are sure that Paul and Silas did not take them down to the river—especially at that unseemly hour—and plunge them into it; for the noble-minded prisoners would not leave the precincts of the jail until they were taken out, in daylight, by proper authority. And it is equally gratuitous and absurd to say there was a bath or tank in the prison, in which the jailer and his family were immersed. A small portion of the water which he brought into the prison to wash the apostle's 'stripes,' was sufficient for his baptism, as, like all the other cases of baptism of which any particulars are given in the New Testament, it was administered by pouring or aspersion." (Summers on Bap., p. 87.)

There is one serious objection to this statement

of the case by Dr. Summers. He and the Scriptures do not agree. I prefer to follow the Word of God. Dr. Summers assumes that the conversion takes place in the jail, that they were baptized in the jail, that a small portion of the water that was brought into the jail to wash the stripes was used for baptizing. That is a very pretty theory if it were true. The Bible reads another way. Here is the way it is recorded in Acts xvi: 27–34: "And the keeper of the prison awaking out of his sleep, and seeing the prison doors open, he drew out his sword, and would have killed himself, supposing that the prisoners had been fled. But Paul cried with a loud voice, saying, 'Do thyself no harm; for we are all here.' Then he called for a light, and sprang in, and came trembling, and fell down before Paul and Silas, *and brought them out*, and said, 'Sirs, what must I do to be saved?' And they said, 'Believe on the Lord Jesus Christ, and thou shalt be saved, and thy house.' And they spake unto him the word of the Lord, *and to all that were in his house* (not in the prison). *And he took them the same hour of the night*, and washed their stripes; and was baptized, he and all of his, straightway. *And when he had brought them into his house*, he set meat before them, and rejoiced, believing in God with all his house."

Nothing is more evident than that the conversion did not take place in the prison, and that the baptism did not take place in either the house or the prison. The Scriptures say this so plainly that there can be no doubt as to the facts in the case. The harmony between our Methodist brother here and the Scriptures is not apparent.

Why was it a thing incredible that Paul and Silas carried this family down "to the river side," and immersed them in the river Strymon, which ran hard by the city? I see nothing impossible or absurd in this. The absurdity rests with the man who does not wish to obey the commandments of our God. The river was there, and if a river is not good for baptismal purposes what is it good for?

There is no doubt that near the house of the jailer there was a suitable place for immersion. Those who know any thing about Eastern houses will have no room to doubt this. Dr. Hibbard, the great Methodist writer on baptism, says, bathing was a custom "indispensable to pleasure, to decency and to health." (Bap., p. 152.) And if this is a fact, is it not likely that the jailer would have had such a place convenient? In this connection the two Episcopalian scholars, Conybeare and Howson, say: "In the same hour of the night the jailer took the Apostles to the well or fountain of water which was within or near the precincts of the prison, and there he washed their wounds, and there he and his household were baptized. He did what he could to assuage the bodily pain of Paul and Silas, and they admitted him and his, by the laver of regeneration, to the spiritual citizenship of the kingdom of God. The prisoners of the jailer had now become his guests." (Life and Epis., p. 267.)

The Scriptures were plain enough that they were not baptized in the jail, but what was to hinder there being a bath in the jail? One of the foremost Pedobaptist scholars in the world has lately made the statement that there was probably a bath in the prison. Prof. Plumptre, in Bishop Ellicott's Commentary, says: "A public prison was likely enough to contain a bath or pool of some kind, where the former (immersion) would be feasible." (Ellicott, Com., vol. 2, p. 109.) I can afford to risk such scholars as Bishop Ellicott and Prof. Plumptre.

I shall use an *ad hominem* argument. Our Methodist and Presbyterian brethren have fully illustrated, in the last few years, the meaning of this scripture. They have repeatedly done the very thing they said could not be done. There are frequent instances where Pedobaptist ministers have immersed persons in jail. What I want to know is this: When was the truth told; when they declared that this thing was absurd and impossible, or when they were immersing persons in the jail after the manner of Paul and and Silas?

I give some examples. Rev. T. T. Eaton, D.D., LL.D., of Louisville, Ky., writes me as follows:

GLOUCESTER, MASS., Aug. 7th, 1890.

DEAR BRO. CHRISTIAN:

Your letter was forwarded to me here. The case of Shade Westmoreland is well known in Chattanooga. I think it was in the spring of 1874 that he was executed. The facts are that he lay in jail in Chattanooga, charged with murder, for fully a year. Once he took an appeal to the supreme court, and they remanded the case to the court below on some point. The court failed to hold a session once on account of the cholera's raging in Chattanooga. That was the summer and fall of 1873. I visited him in jail several times, and talked and prayed with him. At the date of execution I was called to be absent at Hopkinsville, Ky. I bade him good-by, and he expressed regret that I could not "attend to him" at his execution. I told him that any of the ministers would readily be with him, and named Revs. Bachman and Bays. On the morning of the execution they were at the jail,

He asked to be baptized. They were ready to use a pitcher, but he demanded immersion. The jailer was unwilling that he (W.) should be taken to the river, and so Fletcher Rogers soon had a big bath-tub in the jail, and the Revs. J. W. Bachman (Pastor of the Presbyterian Church) and W. W. Bays (Pastor of the Methodist Episcopal Church South) did immerse Shade Westmoreland in the tub in the jail. Bro. Bachman said to me afterwards: "I thought we were giving you an argument when we were doing that." I do not recall the exact date, though that could readily be ascertained from the court records. Hoping this is satisfactory, I am

Yours fraternally, T. T. EATON.

Rev. A. J. Kincaid, of Fort Smith, Ark., writes:

FORT SMITH, ARK., July 30th, 1890.

ELD. J. T. CHRISTIAN, *Jackson, Miss.:*

Dear Brother,—Just about one year ago now, Rev. J. L. Massey, of the M. E. Church of this city, preached a rousing sermon (so he thought) on baptism, in which he seemed to try to annihilate immersion and all who practice it.

In the course of his sermon he said that he had had to perform that indecent act, but that he hoped to God that he would never have it to do again. Through with his tirade on baptism, he came down from his pulpit and offered an opportunity for church-membership, when a lady came to join his church. He received her, and reached for a glass of water, when the lady said to him: "Oh, no, Mr. Massey, that won't do me; you must immerse me." So he had to take her to the Campbellite Church, or to the river—I am not certain which—and immerse her. I think he went with her to the Campbellite Church.

That same week there were several men in the U. S. prison here who were to be hanged. One of them sent for Mr. Massey, and he went to see him and had some religious service with him, and the prisoner professed faith, and wanted to be baptized. The Rev. gentleman called for a cup of water. The prisoner objected, and said that would not do him; that he must put him under the water. In the rear of the prison are some large troughs of water, where he took him and immersed him. It was done in the prison. They have arrangements in the prison yard for the same thing. Indeed it frequently occurs here.

I did not see these things with my own eyes, but I have them from those who did.

Fraternally, A. J. Kincaid.

Rev. J. S. Dill, of Goldsboro, N. C., writes:

GOLDSBORO, N. C., Nov. 1st, 1890.

J. T. CHRISTIAN, D. D.:

My Dear Bro.,—In reply to your inquiry about the jail baptism in Goldsboro I cheerfully certify to the following: One Bud Anderson, having been condemned to be hung for murder, made a profession of faith, and was, in the county jail at Goldsboro, immersed by a Free-will Baptist preacher. The immersion was conveniently performed in a large bath-tub. I visited Mr. Anderson several times, and received from him an account of his baptism. I think the baptism was witnessed by W. R. Parker, then deputy sheriff, and for many years a member of the Missionary Baptist Church. The event occurred in the year 1889.

Fraternally, J. S. DILL,
Pastor Baptist Church.

CHAPTER XIII.
THE ARGUMENT FROM ROM. VI: 4.

"KNOW ye not, that so many of us as were baptized into Jesus Christ were baptized into his death? Therefore we are buried with him by baptism into death: that like as Christ was raised up from the dead by the glory of the Father, even so we also should walk in the newness of life." (Rom. vi: 3, 4. Also Comp. Col. ii: 12.)

There is no more pointed passage in the word of God. This Scripture unquestionably teaches immersion. There is no sort of doubt about it. There is no explanation that could make this passage mean any thing else. It directly refers to the resurrection of Jesus from the grave. As he was buried in the grave so we are buried in the water, and as he arose from the grave so we arise from the watery grave where we have been laid. Our baptism thus becomes a pledge of our future burial and resurrection. It contains in symbol the whole of the Gospel of Christ. Sprinkling and pouring can in no wise symbolize a burial and resurrection. A "drop of water is not as good as an ocean" in this instance. Some of our Pedobaptist brethren try to argue that this refers to a spiritual baptism, and that therefore it does not refer to immersion. I could grant most readily that this passage had reference to a spiritual baptism, and still hold with every degree of reason that it refers to immersion. The spiritual baptism would have an outward symbol or sign, and nothing would more fitly represent this than an immersion in water. This, however, is a mere begging of the question. The scholarship of the world is unanimously opposed to this idea and in favor of a literal baptism. I scarcely know an authority that does not take this view of the subject. The fact is, the scholarship of the world has put this Scripture beyond dispute. This is the one of the few passages that practically all commentators agree as teaching the same thing. I shall give a few of the hundreds of scholars who have written upon this subject. You will see that they reflect the sentiments of all denominations:

Canon Liddon, Episcopalian, on Easter Sunday, 1889, preached a sermon upon "The Likeness of Christ's Resurrection." After showing that Jesus Christ really died upon the cross, the Canon pointed out that according to Paul's teaching the convert to Christianity should really die to sin. "Of this," he proceeded, "the apostle traced the token in the ceremony, at that time universal, of baptism by immersion. As Jesus, crucified and dead, was laid in the grave by Joseph of Arimathea, so the Christian, crucified to the world through the body of Christ descends, as into the tomb, into the baptismal waters. He was buried beneath them; they closed for a moment over him; he was 'planted,' Paul would have said, not only in the likeness of Christ's death, but of his burial. But the immersion is over; the Christian is lifted from the flood, and this evidently corresponded to the resurrection of Christ as the descent had been to his burial. 'Buried with him in baptism wherein ye are also risen with him.'"

John Wesley, Methodist, says: "We are buried with him—alluding to the ancient manner of baptizing by immersion."

Dr. Chalmers, Presbyterian, says: "The original meaning of the word baptism is immersion; and though we regard it as a point of indifferency whether the ordinance so named be performed in this way or by sprinkling, yet we doubt not that the prevalent style of administration in the apostle's days, was by an actual submerging of the body under water. We advert to this, for the purpose of throwing light on the analogy that is instituted in these verses. Jesus Christ, by death, underwent this sort of baptism—even immersion under the surface of the ground, whence he soon emerged again by his resurrection. We, by being baptized into his death, are conceived to have made a similar translation."

Est, Chancellor of the celebrated Catholic University of Douay, says: "For immersion represents to us Christ's burial, and so also his death. For the tomb is a symbol of death, since none but the dead are buried. Moreover, the emersion, which follows the immersion, has a resemblance to the resurrection. We are therefore in baptism conformed not only to the death of Christ, as he has just said, but also to his burial and resurrection."

Meyer, the great German scholar, says: "The recipient of baptism, who by his baptism enters into the fellowship of death with Christ, is necessarily also in the act of baptism ethically buried with him, because after baptism he is spiritually risen with him. In reality this burial with him is not a moral fact distinct from the having died with him, as actual burial is distinct from actual dying; but it sets forth the fullness and completeness of the relation, of which the recipient, in accordance with the form of baptism, so far as the latter takes place through the *katadusin* and *anadusin*, becomes conscious successively. The recipient—thus had Paul figuratively represented the process—is conscious, (*a*) in the baptism *generally:* now I am entered into the fellowship with the death of Christ; (*b*) in *the immersion in particular:* now I am becoming buried with Christ; (*c*) and then in *the emergence:* now I rise to the new life with Christ."

Charles W. Bennett, edited by Bishop John F. Hurst and George R. Crooks, Methodist, says in his new Archæology: "The terms of scripture describing the rite, most of the figures used by the writers of the New Testament to indicate its significance—Rom. vi: 4; Col. ii: 12, etc.—the explanations of the Apostolic Constitutions, the comments of the foremost Christian fathers for the first six centuries, and the express instructions of ecclesiastical councils, indicate that immersion was the more usual mode of baptism."

Adam Clarke, Methodist, says: "It is probable that the Apostle here alludes to the mode of administering baptism by immersion, the whole body being put under water, which seems to say, the man is drowned, is dead; and when he came up out of the water, he seemed to have a resurrection to life, the man is risen again, he is alive."

Albert Barnes, Presbyterian, states: "It is altogether probable that the Apostle in this place had allusion to the custom of baptizing by immersion."

Conybeare and Howson, Episcopalians, say: "This passage can not be understood unless it be borne in mind that the primitive baptism was by immersion." (Life and Epis. p. 557.)

Canon Farrar, Episcopalian, says: "The dipping under the waters of baptism is his union with Christ's death; his rising out of the waters of baptism is a resurrection with Christ, and the birth to a new life." (Life and Works of Paul, p. 362.)

Prof. J. J. Oosterzee, Professor in the University of Utrecht, in his recent work on Christian Dogmatics, vol. 2, p. 749, says: "This sprinkling, which appears to have come first generally into use in the thirteenth century, in place of the entire immersion of the body, in imitation of the previous baptism of the sick, has certainly this imperfection, that the symbolical character of the act is expressed by it much less conspicuously than by complete immersion and burial under water."

I will close this chapter with a statement of Dr. George P. Fisher, Professor of Ecclesiastical History in Yale University, 1887, Beginnings of Christianity, p. 565: "Baptism, it is now generally agreed among scholars, was commonly by immersion."

CHAPTER XIV.

WHAT THE GREEK FATHERS SAY.

NO one doubts that there is much obscurity connected with many of the authors and in the writings of those who are commonly called the fathers. The most remarkable errors are advocated, and the closest discrimination must be used in rating their value. Yet upon the action of baptism we can safely follow them; because this relates to the use of a word and a mere statement of facts. It is not a question of deductions and fancies, but of an act received from the apostles. In this regard their testimony may be regarded highly. I shall not enter into a discussion as to the authenticity of their writings, but set them down as belonging to the years in which they are usually set down by scholars.

Among the so-called Apostolic fathers Barnabas is the only one who speaks of baptism, and his reference is clearly to immersion.

Barnabas, A. D. 119, says: "Blessed are they who, placing their trust in the cross, have gone down into the water; for, says he, they shall receive their reward in due time; then he declares,

I will recompense them. . . . This meaneth, that we indeed descend into the water full of sins and defilement, but come up bearing fruit in our heart, having the fear of God and trust in Jesus in our spirits." (Epis. xi, Ante-Nic. Fath., vol. 1, p. 144.)

Justin Martyr, A. D. 139, is the first who gives a detailed statement of how baptism was performed. We are willing to accept this statement of the act. "I will also relate," says he, "the manner in which we dedicate ourselves to God, where we have been made new through Christ; lest, if we omit this, we seem to be unfair in the explanation we are making, as many as are persuaded and believe that what we teach and say is true, and undertake to be able to live accordingly, are instructed to pray and to entreat God with fasting, for the remission of the sins that are past, we praying and fasting with them. Then they are brought by us where there is water, and are regenerated in the same manner in which we ourselves were regenerated. For in the name of God, the Father, and Lord of the universe, and of our Saviour Jesus Christ, and of the Holy Spirit, they receive the washing with water." (1 Apol. ch. lxi, Ante-Nic. Fath., vol. 1, p. 183.)

This passage unquestionably refers to immersion.

Moses Stuart, the Congregationalist, commenting upon it, says: "I am persuaded that this passage as a whole, most naturally refers to immersion, for why on any other ground should the convert who is to be initiated go out to the place where there is water. There could be no need of this if mere sprinkling, or partial affusion only, was customary in the time of Justin." (On Bap., p. 144.)

Irenæus, A. D. 177, says, speaking of Naaman: "And dipped himself, (says the Scripture,) seven times in Jordan. It was not for nothing that Naaman of old, when suffering from leprosy, was purified upon his being baptized, but (it served) as an indication to us. For as we are lepers in sin, we are made clean, by means of the sacred water, and the invocations of the Lord, from our old transgressions; being spritually regenerated as new born babes, even as the Lord has declared: except a man be born again through the water and the Spirit, he shall not enter the kingdom of heaven." (Frag. 34., Ante-Nic. Fath., vol. 1, p. 574.)

The Pastor of Hermas, A.D. 160, says: "They were obliged to ascend through water in order that they might be made alive; for, unless the deadness of their life was laid aside, they could not in any way enter into the kingdom of God. . . . The seal is the water; they descend into the water dead, and they arise alive." (Sim. ix, ch. xvi, Ante-Nic. Fath., vol. 2, p. 49.)

Origen, A. D. 184—254, says: "The washing in water is the symbol of the purification of the soul cleansed of all impurity of sin." (Com. John, t. viii.) Again, "Man therefore through this washing buried with Christ in regeneration." (Com. Math.)

Hippolytus, A. D. 236, appears as a western preacher speaking and writing in Greek. He says: "Do you see, beloved, how the prophets spake before time of the purifying power of baptism. For he who comes down in faith to the laver of regeneration, and renounces the devil, and joins himself to Christ; who denies the enemy, and makes the confession that Christ is God; who puts off the bondage and puts on the adoption,—he comes up from the baptism as brilliant as the sun, and flashing forth the beams of righteousness, which, indeed, is the chief thing, he returns a son of God and joint heir with Christ." (Holy. Theoph., Ante-Nic. Fath., vol. 5, p. 237.)

Baron Bunsen, who discovered the lost books of Hippolytus, has this to say: "The apostolic church made the school the connecting link between herself and the world. The object of this education was admission into the free society and brotherhood of the church and community. The church adhered rigidly to the principle, as constituting the true import of the baptism ordained of Christ, that no one can be a member of the communion of saints, but by his own free acts and deeds, his own solemn vow made in the presence of the church. It was with this understanding that the candidate for baptism was immersed in water, and admitted as a brother, upon his confession of the Father, the Son, the Holy Ghost." (Hip. His Age, vol. 2, p. 105.)

Gregory Thaumaturgus, A. D. 240, represents Jesus as pleading with John to baptize him in Jordan. He says: "Immerse me in the streams of Jordan, even as she who bore me wrapped me in the children's swaddling clothes. Grant me thy baptism even as the virgin granted me her milk. Lay hold of this head of mine, which the seraphim revere. With thy right hand lay hold on this head, that is related to thyself in kinship. Lay hold of this head, which nature has made to be touched. Lay hold of this head, which for this very purpose has been formed by myself and my Father. Lay hold of this head of mine, which, if any one does lay hold of it in piety, will save him from ever suffering shipwreck. Baptize me, who am destined to baptize those who believe on me with water, and with the Spirit, and with fire; with water capable of washing away the defilement of sins; with the Spirit, capable of making the earthly spiritual; with fire, naturally fitted to consume the thorns of transgressions. On learning these words, the Baptist directed his mind to the object of the salvation, and comprehended the mystery which he had received, and discharged the divine command; for he was at once pious and ready to obey, and stretching forth slowly his right hand, which seemed both to tremble and to rejoice, he baptized the Lord." (Four Hom. Ante-Nic. Fath., vol. 6, p. 70.)

Chrysostom, 347, says: "To be baptized and to submerge, then to emerge, is a symbol of descent to the grave, and of ascent from it." (Hom. 40 in 1 Cor. i.) Again he says: "We, as in a sepulcher, immersing our heads in water, the old man is buried, and sinking down, the hole is covered at once; then as we emerge, the new man rises again." (Cap. iii, Johanis.)

Dionysius says: "Properly the total covering by water is taken from an image of death and burial out of sight." (Areop. di Eccl. Heir. c. 2.)

Basil, A. D. 330, says: "By the three immersions, and by the like number of invocations, the great mystery of baptism is completed." (De Spirtu, c. 15.)

CHAPTER XV.

WHAT THE LATIN FATHERS SAY.

THE testimony of the Latin fathers is equally as conclusive as that of the Greeks. I begin with Tertullian, A. D. 150, the oldest of the Latin fathers. He makes frequent reference to baptism. He says: "When entering the water, we make profession of the Christian faith in the words of its rule; we bear public testimony that we have renounced the devil, his pomp and his angels." (De Spec. ch. iv.) Again, "To deal," says he, "with this matter briefly, I shall begin with baptism. When we are going to enter the water, but a little before, in the presence of the congregation and under the hand of the president, we solemnly profess that we disown the devil, and his pomp and his angels. Thereupon we are thrice immersed, making a somewhat ampler pledge than the Lord has appointed in the Gospel. Then we are taken up (as new born children)." (De Corona ch. iii.) Against Marcion, ch. xxviii, he says: "He therefore seals man, who had never been unsealed in respect of him; washes man who had never been defiled so far as he was concerned; and into this sacrament of salvation wholly plunges that flesh which is beyond the pale of salvation." On the Resurrection, ch. xlii, he says: "Know ye not, that so many of us as are dipped into Jesus Christ, are baptized into his death. We are, therefore, buried with him by baptism into death, that just as Christ was raised up from the dead, even so we also should walk in newness of life." Tertullian has also written a treatise on baptism. He says, ch. iv: "And accordingly it makes no difference whether a man be washed in a sea or a pool, a stream or a fount, a lake or a trough; nor is there any distinction between those whom John baptized in the Jordan and those whom Peter baptized in the Tiber, unless withal the Eunuch whom Philip baptized in the midst of his journeys with chance water, derived (therefrom) more or less of salvation than others." On Bap. ch. xiii, he says: "For the law of dipping has been imposed, and the formula prescribed: Go, he saith, teach the nations, dipping them into the name of the Father, and of the Son, and of the Holy Spirit."

So manifestly does Tertullian teach immersion that Dr. George Campbell does not hesitate to state: "The word *baptizein*, both in sacred authors, and in classical, signifies to dip, to plunge, to immerse, and was rendered by Tertullian, the oldest of the Latin Fathers, tingere; the term used for dyeing cloth, which was by immersion." (Four Gos. vol. 4, p. 24.) And Moses Stuart remarks: "I do not see how any doubt can well remain, that in Tertullian's time the practice of the African church, to say the least, as to the mode of baptism, must have been that of trine immersion." On Bapt. p. 146.)

Cyprian, A. D. 250, Epis. xxiv, renders the commission: "The Lord, when after his resurrection he sent forth his apostles, charges them saying, all power is given unto me in heaven and in earth. Go ye, therefore, and teach all nations, dipping them into the name of the Father, and of the Son, and of the Holy Ghost; teaching them to observe all things whatsoever I have commanded you." And quoting Gal. iii: 27, Epis. 75, he says: "For if the apostle does not speak falsely when he says, As many of you as are dipped into Christ have put on Christ, certainly he who has been baptized among them into Christ, has put on Christ."

Ambrose, Bishop of Milan, A. D. 340, says: "Thou wast asked, Dost thou believe in God the Father Almighty. Thou saidst, I believe, and thus thou wast immersed, that is, wast buried." (Sacram. Lit. ii, c. 7.)

The great Augustine says: "After you professed your belief three times, did we submerge your heads in the sacred fountain." (Hom. iv.) "Rightly," says he, in another place, "are ye immersed three times, who have received baptism in the name of Christ. . . . . For that thrice repeated submersion expresses a resemblance of the Lord's death."

Jerome, A. D. 331, says: "And thrice were we immersed, that there may appear one sacrament of the Trinity." (Epis. ad Eph. ch. iv.)

Alcuin, A. D. 735, to the brethren at Lyons, Epis. xc, writes: "To us it seems indeed, according to our feeble judgment, that as the inner man is formed anew after the image of his Maker, in the faith of the Holy Trinity, so the outer man should be washed with a trine immersion; that what the Spirit invisibly works in the soul, that the priest may visibly imitate in water." In describing the act of baptism he says: "And so, in the name of the holy Trinity, he is baptized by trine immersion." (Epis. xc. col. 292.)

There can remain no question from these extracts that the early Latin fathers taught immersion as the act of Christian baptism. For the first time, in the writings of Tertullian, we cross trine immersion. He expressly says, however, that this "is somewhat more than the Lord prescribed in the Gospel." Jerome also states that trine baptism is only a matter of tradition. "Many of the things," says Jerome, "which are observed in the churches by tradition, have usurped to themselves the authority of the written law (of the Scriptures); such as to immerse the head three times in the bath." (Advers. Lucif. c. 4.) But the act of baptism, which is by immersion, remains untouched. The fathers are unanimous in favor of dipping.

CHAPTER XVI.

"THE TEACHING OF THE TWELVE APOSTLES."

IN 1884 a translation of this work was given to the English-speaking world by Archdeacon Farrar. It had been discovered by Bryennios in 1873, and an edition of it printed by him in 1883. It bore a very significant signature—"Leon, Notary and Sinner"—and the Greek date 6564, which equals 1056. It at once created the wildest enthusiam among our Pedobaptist friends. The Baptist position was certainly overthrown, and our position was utterly untenable! Yet out of this very thing has come a great good to the Baptists. "The Teaching" has caused unlimited discussion, and every agitation of the baptismal question is to our advantage. We have every thing to gain when this subject is stirred. After seven years the sweep of scholarship is all toward immersion, and we are more firmly implanted in our position than ever before.

The famous chapter that was relied on to do such wonderful things is found in the Constantinople edition, pp. 27–29, and is translated by Dr. Schaff as follows: "Now concerning baptism, baptize thus:

Having first taught all these things, baptize ye in the name of the Father, and of the Son, and of the Holy Ghost, in living water. And if thou hast not living water, baptize in other water; and if thou canst not in cold, then in warm (water). But if thou hast neither, pour (water) thrice upon the head in the name of the Father, and of the Son, and of the Holy Ghost. But before baptism let the baptizer and the baptized fast, and any others who can; but thou shalt command the baptizer to fast for one or two days before."

I will make several interesting observations:

1. This is undoubtedly a very great variation from the teaching of the New Testament; and it matters not what this book says, the New Testament is the standard of authority. The New Testament nowhere calls baptism *ekcheo*, to pour; it is always *baptizo*, to dip. This alone stamps this book of late origin.

2. Immersion is plainly preferred, and pouring is only allowed in the extreme cases, and that must be performed three times. As Dr. Schaff remarks: "The preference of the ante-Nicene church was for baptism in a running stream, as the Jordan, the Nile, the Tiber." (Teaching, p. 185.)

3. Fasting is as fully and emphatically taught as is pouring; indeed the injunction is absolute.

4. There are some other very fatal objections to pedobaptism in this book: (1.) Infant baptism is left out of the "Teaching." In trying to overthrow immersion, infant baptism is destroyed. Instruction is positively enjoined before baptism, and this forever excludes infant baptism. Dr. Schaff admits that "infant baptism is not contemplated in the Didache." (2.) This book teaches the Baptist doctrine of close communion. No one but baptized persons must come to the table of the Lord. Chapter ix commands that, "Let no one eat or drink of the Eucharist except those baptized into the name of the Lord." Our Presbyterian brother, Dr. Schaff, is still giving us good testimony. He says: "The communion is for baptized believers, and for them only. Baptism is the sacramental sign and seal of regeneration and conversion; the Lord's Supper is the sacrament of sanctification and growth in spiritual grace. . . . Hence the Apostolic Constitutions lay great stress on the exclusion of unbelievers from the Eucharist." (Teaching, p. 193.) (3.) The Teaching is also fatal to the doctrine of Episcopacy, for only two classes of officers are recognized—Bishops and Deacons. These are to be elected by the people. The Greek verb means, in classical writers, to stretch out the hand, or to vote by show of hands; then to elect. This

is rather a discouraging view of the matter to our Pedobaptist friends.

5. The book is full of all kinds of childish twaddle. The truth is that it is supremely silly in many places. Concerning the character of the work, Bishop Cleveland Coxe in his prefatory note says: "Even Lactantius, in his Institutes, shapes his instructions to Constantine by the *Dua Via*, which seemed to have been formulated in the earliest ages for the training of catechumens. The elementary nature and 'the childishness' of the work are thus accounted for, and I am sure that the 'Mystagogic' teaching of Cyril receives light from this view of the matter. This work was food for 'lambs'; it was not meant to meet the wants of those 'of full age.' It may prove, as Dr. Riddle hints, that the *Teaching*, as we have it in the Bryennios document, is tainted by the views of some nascent sect or heresy, or by the incompetency of some obscure local church as yet unvisited by learned teachers and evangelists. It seems to me not improbably influenced by views of the *charismata*, which ripened into Montanism, and which are illustrated by the warnings and admonitions of Hermas." (Ante-Nicene Fathers, vol. 7, p. 171.)

Those who wish to follow this mixture of foolishness and heresy can do so, but I prefer the word of the living God as my counselor.

6. The morality of the book is positively shocking. The very first chapter teaches that if a man is in need and steals it is all right. Hear it: "Woe to him that taketh; for if one that is in need taketh, he shall be guiltless; but he that is not in need shall give account whereof he took and whereunto; and being in durance shall be questioned touching what he did, and he shall not go out thence until he give back the last farthing." I am very glad we do not have to defend immersion with such stuff as this.

7. The truth is that no two writers agree in regard to scarcely any particulars concerning this book. There are the wildest and most absurd contradictions in regard to the writer, the time it was written, the country, and almost every detail connected with the work. Prof. Harnack, who first announced this book to the Western World, and who has studied it more closely than any other, has furnished a series of articles for the *Theologische Literaturzeitung*. What we give below was published June, 12th, 1886, and republished in the New York *Independent* Aug. 26th, 1886. It put together, without comment, the conflicting opinions that are held in regard to it. Dr. Harnack says:

"One investigator puts the newly discovered writing before the Pauline letters, or even before the council of the apostles (Sabatier); the second, in the time of Paul; the third, soon after the destruction of Jerusalem (Bestinann); the fourth, in the last decades of the first century (an idea that finds very much favor); the fifth, in the days of Trajan (also a favorite idea); the sixth, in the days of Barcochba; the seventh, in the time of Antonines; the eighth, about the time of Commodus; the ninth, in the third century; the tenth, in the fourth century; and there are some who favor the fifth or a later century. So much in reference to the time of composition.

"In other points matters stand no better. On the history of its transmission one says that it is the book known to the Fathers from the days of Clement; others deny this; a third party seeks a middle path in regard to the integrity of the book; some say the book is from one author, and original; others that it is a compilation, and is crowded with interpolations; that it consists of two or more parts that originally did not belong together. In regard to the character of the book, some claim that it is well arranged, others that it is poorly arranged; some that in parts it is well arranged, and in parts poorly arranged; some that the skill of the author must be admired; others that the author has no idea of the literary arts.

"With regard to the sources, some say that only the old Testament served as a source, and that all the rest is original, because older than all other Christian writings; others say that there is nothing original in the book, but the whole is taken from other sources; some that the new Testament receives no witness from the Didache; others that nearly all the New Testament books are used in it, and that the book itself thereby seems the best proof of its antiquity; some that Barnabas and Hermas are used; others that Barnabas is used, but that Hermas in turn used the 'Didache'; others, on the other hand, that Hermas was used, and that Barnabas is a later production; others that Philo, the Sybiline books, and the Gentile moralists were used; others that in primitive apostolic simplicity the author has reproduced only the pure Gospel.

"In regard to the standpoint of the author, some claim that it is primitive-apostolic from the view of the Jewish Christians; others, that it is post-apostolic and Jewish-Christian; others, anti-Pauline; others, that it is strongly influenced by Paul; others, that it is Saddusaic; others, vulgar, heathenish; others, dangerously Ebionitic; others, Marcionitic; others, Montanistic; others, Theodosian; others, quite moralizing; others, encratistic; others, thoroughly Byzantine, but under a transparent mask; others, that the standpoint can not be discovered, since the author has not treated of his faith; others, classically evangelical.

"With regard to the importance of the book, some say that it is the most important discovery of the century, and should be received into the canon of the New Testament; that it is the whole Bible in *nuce;* that it solves the greatest problems; that it is peculiar, and should be used with care; that it shows the average Christianity; that as a compilation it can not be used in picturing any period; that it shows poverty of contents; the Christianity of the author can only be lamented; that it is rationalistic and flat, but nevertheless interesting; that it is a miserable production, without any importance for those of our times; the book is characteristic only of the Byzantine forger. Places assigned for the writing: Egypt, Greece, Syria, Jerusalem, Rome, Asia Minor, Constantinople.

"Then some regard it as setting forth the apostolic, the Presbyterian, the Episcopal, or no system of church government whatever. It is considered of great value because it favors the Protestant, or the Catholic, or the Baptist, or the anti-Baptist, or the Chiliastic, or the anti-Chiliastic, or the Irvingian, or some other church party; because it is still apostolic and anti-Catholic and at the same time Catholic; because its prophets are still apostles of the real primitive Christianity; others, then, claim that they are new prophets, or no prophets at all, but rather inventive swindlers and parasites; others, that they are no swindlers, but *homunculi* produced by a forger."

I have given this full discussion of this work on account of the prominence given to the Teaching in so many quarters. It will easily be seen that scholars must come nearer to an agreement before the work can be seriously quoted as an authority. Granting the extremest position of our opponents, we gain by the book quite as much as we lose. The truth is that the part that may appear to favor the Pedobaptists is really the part that is directly against the teaching of the New Testament.

CHAPTER XVII.

ARGUMENT FROM HISTORY IN FAVOR OF IMMERSION.

ALL standard historians, regardless of denomination, assert that immersion was the primitive act of baptism. Time would fail me to give them all, for their name is legion. I will content myself, therefore, by making such selections as I may deem best.

As the first authority I will give Dr. Arthur P. Stanley, a late dignitary of the Church of England. He was the son of a bishop. He was for seven years Professor of Ecclesiastical History in Oxford University. He is the author of several works of high critical value, and stood at the head of English scholars. His last position was Lord Rector of St. Andrew's and Dean of Westminster Abbey. He says of baptism: "Into this society they passed by an act as natural as it was expressive. The plunge into the bath of purification, long known among the Jewish nation as the symbol of a change of life, had been revived with a fresh energy by the Essenes, and it received a definite signification and impulse from the austere prophet who derived his name from the ordinance. This rite was retained as the pledge of entrance into a new and universal communion. In that early age the scene of the transaction was either some deep wayside spring or well, as for the Ethiopian, or some rushing river, as the Jordan, or some vast reservoir, as at Jericho or Jerusalem, whither, as in the baths of Caracalla at Rome, the whole population resorted for swimming or washing. The earliest scene of the immersion was in the Jordan. That rushing river—the one river of Palestine—found at last its fit purpose." (Christian Institutions, p. 2.)

Dr. Adolf Harnack, of Giessen, the foremost living German Church historian, in reply to some questions of C. E. W. Dobbs, D. D., made the following statement on "the present state of opinion among German scholars," concerning the ancient act of baptism:

GIESSEN, Jan. 16th, 1885.

C. E. W. DOBBS, D. D.:

Dear Sir,—Referring to your three inquiries, I have the honor to reply:

1st. Baptism undoubtedly signifies immersion, (*eintauchen.*)

2d. No proof can be found that it signifies any thing else in the New Testament, and in the most ancient Christian literature. The suggestion regarding "a sacred sense," is out of the question.

3d. There is no passage in the New Testament which suggests the supposition that any New Testament author attached to the word *baptizein* any other sense than *eintauchen=untertauchen*." (Schaff's Teach. of the Twelve, p. 50.)

Dr. Joseph Langen, Old Catholic Professor in Bonn, Germany, in a letter to myself, in April, of this year, says: "In reply to your pleasing letter of March 13th, I have to say the following:

"1. The meaning of the word *baptizein* is to dip under.

"2. The authors of the New Testament have never used the word in any other sense.

"3. In Western countries not till after the eleventh century, after the separation from the East, was pouring on the head generally established in the place of dipping under."

Dr. Philip Schaff, the eminent Presbyterian scholar and historian, of New York, says: "The usual form of baptism was by immersion. This is inferred from the original of the Greek *baptizein* and *baptismos;* from the analogy of John's baptism in the Jordan; from the apostle's comparison of the sacred rite with the miraculous passage of the Red Sea, and the escape of the ark from the flood, with a cleansing and refreshing bath, and with burial and resurrection; finally, from the general custom of the ancient church, which prevails in the East to this day." (Christ. Ch., vol. 1, pp. 468, 469.)

Homersham Cox, a very learned English judge, says in his recent book, The First Century of Christianity: "The Jews baptized by immersion, and this was undoubtedly the form of the Christian institution originally, though subsequently baptism by affusion was allowed. Even so late as the age of Cyprian (the third century) this method, though tolerated, was not the most usual." (p. 227.)

George P. Fisher, Professor of Ecclesiastical History in Yale University, says: "Baptism, it is now generally agreed among scholars, was commonly by immersion." (Begin. Christ. p. 565.)

Prof. L. L. Paine, D. D., of the Bangor Theological Seminary, some time since surprised some of his friends by teaching that immersion was baptism, and he wrote the following in his own justification: "It may be honestly asked by some, Was immersion the primitive form of baptism, and, if so, what then? As to the question of fact, the testimony is ample and decisive. No matter of Church history is clearer. The evidence is all one way, and all church historians of any repute agree in accepting it. We can not even claim originality in teaching it in a Congregational Seminary. And we really feel guilty of a kind of anachronism in writing an article to insist upon it. It is a point on which ancient, mediæval and modern historians alike, Catholic and Protestant, Lutheran and Calvinist, have no controversy. And the simple reason for this unanimity, is that the statements of the early fathers are so clear, and the light shed upon their statements from the early customs of the church, is so conclusive, that no historian who cares for his reputation would dare to deny it, and no historian who is worthy of the name would wish to. There are some historical questions concerning the early church, on which the most learned writers disagree—for example the question of infant baptism; but on this one of the early practice of immersion, the most distinguished antiquarians, such as Bingham, Augusti, Coleman, Smith, and historians such as Mosheim, Gieseler, Hase, Milman, Schaff, Alzog (Catholic) hold a common language."

What is more, scholars of the highest repute state that immersion was the common act of baptism for thirteen hundred years. This is a very strong point, and I will let the scholars speak for themselves.

Dr. H. Holtzmann, Professor in Strasburg University, writes me April 4th, 1890: "The meaning of the word *baptizein*, as of the simple *baptein*, is to 'dip in, to dip under.' At a later date, instead of immersion, aspersion occurs in the cases of sickness, and was called clinic baptism. Aspersion became only more common in consequence of the baptism of children, and never obtained a meaning similar to immersion until after the thirteenth century."

Dr. Hilgenfeld, Professor in the University of Jena, writes me: "Only in the Western Church, and after the thirteenth century, did sprinkling come in as the usual mode of baptism, so that it became the general custom in the fourteenth century. The baptism by immersion, however, is still preserved by the Greek Catholic Church."

Prof. Gaston Bonet-Maury, Professor in the Protestant Theological Faculty of Paris, writes: "The literal meaning of the Greek word *baptizein* is to plunge, to immerse, to dip. Baptism by immersion is still practiced by all the orthodox Greek churches of the East. This form was practiced in the West until the close of the thirteenth century. But at the close of the thirteenth century, baptism by aspersion prevailed definitely for the baptism of children. In 1311 the Council of Ravenna allowed free choice between immersion and aspersion. Thomas Aquinas declares the two forms equally legitimate. Baptism by immersion has been preserved until the present time in the cathedral of Milan. In the sixteenth century Edward VI. and Queen Elizabeth were baptized by immersion, and the English liturgy of baptism enjoined immersion for the public baptism of little children. Since the beginning of the seventeenth century this form has been very rare in the non-Baptist churches."

Dr. Philip Schaff, Presbyterian, says: " Pouring and sprinkling were still exceptional in the ninth century, according to Walafrid Strabo (De Rel. Eccl. c. 26); but they made gradual progress, with the spread of infant baptism, as the most convenient mode, especially in northern climates, and came into common use in the West at the end of the thirteenth century."

Dollinger, the eminent Catholic author who so recently died at Bonn, says in his History: "Baptism by immersion continued to be the prevailing practice of the Church as late as the fourteenth century." (Hist. Ch. vol. 2, p. 294.)

Dean Stanley says: "For the first thirteen centuries the almost universal practice of baptism was that of which we read in the New Testament, and which is the very meaning of the word 'baptize'—that those who were baptized were plunged, submerged, immersed into the water. That practice is still, as we have seen, continued in Eastern churches." (Chris. Ins. p. 17.)

Dr. Funk, of Tubingen University, writes that, "In the thirteenth century the practice of pouring began considerably to prevail; and in some places (as in France) somewhat earlier than this."

Here are seven witnesses—and many more might be given—all testifying that immersion was the common practice for thirteen hundred years. They say it was the universal practice, save those who were baptized upon their sick-bed. Could I want stronger testimony to the primitive rite? These men are Presbyterians, Catholics, and Episcopalians, and are not prejudiced toward the Baptists. The testimony is sure, and our position remains tenable. The voice of history is fully on our side, and all antiquity says that the ancient act of baptism was an immersion in water.

CHAPTER XVIII.

SPRINKLING A HEATHEN CUSTOM.

THE practice of sprinkling, for baptism, is of pagan origin. In the days of the apostles corrupt practices began to creep into the churches. In the course of time, as the Roman Catholic Church began to extend its borders, thousands of baptized, but unconverted heathen, were received into her communion. These persons assumed the name of Christians, but brought along with them their corrupt and abominable practices. They changed their name, but not their rites and ceremonies. One of the doctrines they brought with them was that of baptismal salvation. This has been the bane of pure Christianity. But along with this came the attendant evils of sprinkling and infant baptism. The heathens worshiped the river as a god, and believed that a bath in its waters, or its sacred water poured or sprinkled upon themselves, would bring everlasting life. It was a matter of indifference to them how the water should be applied.

With the corruptions of Christianity this idea began to prevail among the thousands who came from the heathen. The argument was to them complete and convincing: If water baptism saved a man, and this many of the fathers most ardently believed, it was very necessary that a man should not die without the "laver of regeneration." But as it is not always convenient to dip a man who was at the point of death, copious pouring was resorted to as in the case of Novatian; and from this confessed innovation, sprinkling has become the general practice of the Roman Catholic Church, and of those churches which have been connected with it. The same matter of convenience and salvation applied to infants, and so it became customary to sprinkle them in case they were weak, and from that came the prevailing custom of infant sprinkling. If there was no such doctrine as baptismal salvation, infant baptism would die a natural death, and sprinkling would never have been a custom in the Christian world.

But I will make good these statements that baptismal salvation and affusion are of heathen origin, and have been engrafted as a custom upon the Christian religion. These propositions will more fully appear from the unimpeachable authorities that I present. I wish especially to acknowledge my indebtedness to a very able editorial which appeared in the January number, 1891, of the *Outlook*.

The pagans were accustomed to worship the sun, rivers and fountains, and sometimes their rites were a combination of ceremonies to these. It is in this way that Virgil writes:

"He started up, and viewing the rising beams of the ethereal sun, in his hollow palms, with pious form, he raised water from the river, and poured forth to heaven these words: Ye nymphs, ye Laurentine nymphs, whence rivers have their origin; and thou, O Father Tiber, with thy sacred river; receive Æneas and defend him at length from dangers. In whatever source thy lake contains thee, compassionate to our misfortunes, from whatever soil thou springest forth most beauteous, horn-bearing river, monarch of the Italian streams, ever shalt thou be honored with my veneration, ever with my offerings. O grant us thy present aid, and by nearer aid confirm thy divine oracles." (Æneid, b. 8, l. 70–82.)

Ovid, describing the feast of Pales, held in May, exhibits the same combination of sun and water worship:

"Often in truth have I leaped over the fires placed in three rows, and the dripping bough of laurel has flung the sprinkled waters. . . .

Shepherd, purify the full sheep at the beginning of twilight, let the water first sprinkle them, and let the broom made of twigs sweep the ground. . . . Protect thou alike the cattle, and let all harm fly away, repelled from my stalls. Let that happen which I pray for, and may we at the close of the year, offer cakes of good size to Pales, the mistress of the shepherds. With these words must the goddess be propitiated; turning to the East, do you repeat these words three times, and in the running stream thoroughly wash your hands." (Fasti, bk. 4, l. 728–779.)

In another place Ovid tells us of Deucalion and Phyrra, resolving to seek the sacred oracles, in prayer, at the temple of the goddess Themis; he says:

"There is no delay; together they repair to the waters of Cephsius, though not clear, yet now cutting their wonted channel. Then when they had sprinkled the waters poured on their clothes and their heads, they turn their steps to the temple of the sacred goddess, the roof of which was defiled with foul moss, and whose altars were standing without fires." (Metamorphoses, bk. 1, fable 10, lines 651, &c.)

Sir Monier-Williams, describing water worship, and one of the temples in India, says:

"Thither, therefore, a constant throng of worshippers continually resort, bringing with them offerings of flowers, rice and other grains, which they throw into the water thirty or forty feet below the ground. A Brahman is perpetually employed in drawing up the putrid liquid, the smell, or rather stench of which, from incessant admixture of decaying flowers and of vegetable matter, making the neighborhood almost unbearable. This he pours with a ladel into the hands of the expectant crowd, who either drink it with avidity, or sprinkle it reverentially over their persons. A still more sacred well called the Manikarnika, situated on one of the chief Ghats leading to the Ganges, owes its origin, in popular belief, to the fortunate circumtance that one of Siva's ear-rings happened to fall on the spot. This well is near to the surface and quite exposed to view. It forms a small quadrangular pool, not more than three feet deep. Four flights of steps on the four sides lead to the water, the disgusting foulness of which, in the estimation of countless pilgrims, vastly enhances its efficacy for the removal of sin. The most abandoned criminals journey from the most distant parts of India to the margin of this sacred pool. There they secure the services of Brahmins, appointed to the duty, and descending with them into the water, are made to repeat certain texts and mutter certain mystic formulæ, the meaning of which they are wholly unable to understand. Then, while in the act of repeating the words put into their mouths, they eagerly immerse their entire persons beneath the offensive liquid. The long looked for dip over, a miraculous transformation is the result; for the foul water has cleansed the still fouler soul. Few Hindus venture to doubt that the most depraved sinner in existence may thus be converted into an immaculate saint, worthy of being translated at once to the highest heavens of the God of Benares." (Brahminism and Hinduism by Sir Monier-Williams, M. A., D. C. L., London 1887.)

In a still later work, Sir William describes the present baptismal custom in Thibet and Mongolia, as follows:

"It is noticeable that a kind of infant baptism is practiced in Thibet and Mongolia. It is usual to sprinkle children with consecrated water, or to immerse them entirely on the third or tenth day after birth. This is called khrus-sol (according to Jaschke). The priest consecrates the water by reciting some formula, while candles and incense are burning. He then dips the child three times, blesses it, and gives it a name. After performing the ceremony he draws up the infant's horoscope. Then as soon as the child can walk and talk, a second ceremony takes place, and prayers are said for its happy life, and an amulet or little bag is hung around its neck, filled with spells and charms against evil spirits and diseases." (Buddhism, etc.)

Alabaster also says:

"Baptism was a religious rite from very ancient times, the Brahmins holding that if any one who had sinned went to the banks of the Ganges and saying, 'I will not sin again,' plunged into the stream, he would rise to surface free of sin, all his floating away. Sometimes when any one was sick unto death, his relatives would place him by the river, and give him water to drink, and pour water over him till he died, believing that he would thus die holy and go to heaven." (Buddhism, pp. 30, 31.)

Mallet says of baptism in Scandinavia:

"It was no less remarkable that a kind of infant baptism was practiced in the North, long before the dawning of Christianity, and had reached those parts. Snorri Sturlason, in his chronicle, speaking of a Norwegian noble who lived in the reign of Harold Harfragra, relates that he poured water on the head of a new born child, and called him Hakon, from the name of his father. Harald himself had been baptized in the same manner, and it is noted of King Olaf Tryggvason, that his mother Astrida had him thus baptized and named as soon as he was born. The Livonians observed the same ceremony, which also prevailed among the Germans, as appears from a letter which the famous Pope Gregory the Third sent to their Apostle Boniface, directing expressly how to act in this respect. It is probable that all of these people might intend, by such a rite, to preserve their children from the sorceries and evil charms which wicked spirits might employ against them at the instant of their birth. Several nations of Asia and America have attributed such a power to ablutions of this kind; nor were the Romans without such a custom, though they did not wholly confine it to new born infants." (Mallett's Scandinavian, p. 206.)

S. Baring Gould testifies concerning pagan baptisms in Scandinavia as follows:

"Among the Scandinavians, infant baptism was in vogue before the introduction of Christianity, and the rite accompanied the naming of the child. Before the accomplishment of this rite, the exposition of the babe was lawful, but after the ceremony it became murder. A baptism in blood seems to have been practiced by the Germans and Norsemen in remote antiquity; to this the traditions of the horny Sigfrid, or Sigurd, and Wolfdietrich point. Dipping in water, and aspersion with water, or with the blood of a victim, was also customary among the Druids, as was also the baptism of Fire, perhaps borrowed by them from the Phœnicians. This was that passing through the fire to Molech alluded to repeatedly in the Jewish Scriptures." (Orig. and Devel. Rel. Bel. Circu. p. 397.)

Prescott speaks of the amazement with which the early Spaniards beheld the points of similarity between the customs of the Pagan Mexicans and the Roman Catholic Church: He says:

"With the same feelings they witnessed another ceremony, that of the Aztec baptism; in which, after a solemn invocation, the head and lips of the infant were touched with water, and a name given to it; while the goddess Cioacoati, who presided over child-birth, was implored that the sin which was given to us before the beginning of the world, might not visit the child, but that, cleansed by these waters, it might live and be born anew." (Con. of Mex. vol. 3, p. 369.)

A full account of these pagan baptisms in Mexico is given by Shagun-de-Bernardino, as follows:

"When every thing necessary for the baptism had been made ready, all the relations of the child were assembled, and the midwife, who was the person that performed the rite of baptism, was summoned. At early dawn they met together in the court-yard of the house. When the sun had risen, the midwife, taking the child in her arms, called for a little earthen vessel of water, while those about her placed the ornaments which had been prepared for the baptism in the midst of the court. To perform the rite of baptism, she placed herself with her face toward the west, and immediately began to go through certain ceremonies. After this she sprinkled water on the head of the infant, saying, 'O my child, take and receive the water of the Lord of the world, which is our life, and is given for the increasing and renewing of our body. It is to wash and to purify. I pray that these heavenly drops may enter into your body and dwell there; that they may destroy and remove from you all the evil and sin which was given to you before the beginning of the world; since all of us are under its power, being all the children of Chalchivitlycue' (the goddess of water). She then washed the body of the child with water, and spoke in this manner: 'Whencesoever thou comest, thou that art hurtful to this child, leave him and depart from him, for he now liveth anew, and is born anew; now he is purified, and cleansed afresh. And our mother Chalchivitlycue again bringeth into the world.' Having thus prayed, the midwife took the child in both hands, lifted him toward heaven, and said: 'O Lord, thou seest here thy creature, whom thou hast sent into this world, this place of sorrow, suffering, and penitence. Grant him, O Lord, thy gifts and thine inspiration, for thou art the great God, and with thee is the great goddess.' Torches of pine were kept burning during the performance of these ceremonies. When these things were ended they gave the child the name of some one of his ancestors, in hope that he might shed a new luster over it. The name was given by the same midwife or priestess who baptized him." (Hist. de Neuva-Espana, lib. 6, cap. 37.)

From these unimpeachable authorities nothing is more evident than that the heathens believed in baptismal salvation, and practiced infant baptism, and that the act was pouring, sprinkling, and immersion indifferently. When some of the popular Church Liturgies of to-day are compared with the prayers and performances quoted above, the similarity is most striking and startling. The truth is that the ceremonies of infant sprinkling are taken from the Elusinian and Druidical lustrations. Many of the foremost Pedobaptist scholars do not deny, but freely admit, this fact.

Dr. Bennett, a Methodist author whom we have frequently quoted, repeatedly shows that in the architecture of the third and following centuries heathen thought and figures are used, and that a heathen god is in the only picture of pouring for baptism found in early art. His whole book on "Archæology" is a statement of this fact.

Dean Stanley is even more explicit. He says: "*It is astonishing* how many of these decorations are taken from heathen sources and copied from heathen paintings. There is Orpheus playing on his harp to the beasts; there is Bacchus as the god of the vintage; there is Psyche, the butterfly of the soul; there is the Jordan as the god of the river. The Classical and the Christian, the Hebrew and the Hellenic, elements had not yet parted. The strict demarkation, which the books of the period would imply, between the Christian Church and the heathen world, had not yet been formed, or was constantly effaced. The Catacombs had more affinity with the chapel of Alexander Severus, which contained Orpheus side by side with Abraham and Christ, than they have with the writings of Tertullian, who spoke of heathen poets only to exult in their future torments; or of Augustine, who regarded this very figure of Orpheus only as a mischievous teacher to be disparaged, not as a type of the two forms of heathen and Christian civilization. It agrees with the fact that the funeral inscriptions are often addressed *Dis manibus,* 'to the funeral spirits.'" (Inst. p. 230.)

If any thing more was needed, the statement of the late Cardinal Newman would put it at rest when he speaks of these appendages as "the very instruments and appendages of demon worship." (Devel. pp. 359, 360.)

In truth the Roman Catholic writers defended it as the very best policy possible. No man is higher authority among Roman Catholics than Cardinal Baronius. He says:

"It was permitted the Church to transfer to pious uses those ceremonies which the pagans had wickedly applied in a superstitious worship, after having purified them by consecration; so that, to the greater contumely of the devil, all might honor Christ with those rites which he intended for his own worship. Thus the pagan festivals, laden with superstition, were changed into praiseworthy festivals of the martyrs; and the idolatrous temples were changed to sacred churches, as Theodoret shows."

The scholarly Max Muller says of the first three centuries:

"This age was characterized, far more than all

before it, by a spirit of religious syncretism, an eager thirst for compromise. To mold together thoughts which differed fundamentally, to grasp, if possible, the common elements pervading all the multifarious religions of the world, was deemed the proper business of philosophy, both in the East and in the West. It was a period, one has lately said, of mystic incubation, when India and Egypt, Babylon and Greece, were sitting together and gossiping like crazy old women, chattering with toothless gums and silly brains about the dreams and joys of their youth, yet unable to recall one single thought or feeling with that vigor which once gave it light and truth.

"It was a period of religious and metaphysical delirium, when every thing became every thing; when Maya and Sophia, Mithra and Christ, Viraf and Isaiah, Belus, Zarvan, and Kronos were mixed up in one jumbled system of inane speculation, from which at least the East was delivered by the positive doctrines of Mohammed, the West by the pure Christianity of the Teutonic nations." (Last Res. of Persian Res. c. 3, sec. 1, part 1.)

I would, therefore, state the case thus: In the New Testament we find no such things as baptismal salvation, infant baptism, sprinkling and pouring, godfathers, and many more such things;

but in contemporary heathenism we will find all of these things. A little later there are thousands of baptized but unconverted heathen received into the Church. They were required to change their name, but not their practices. It came to pass that all of these ceremonies found in heathenism, but unknown in the New Testament, were found in the Catholic Church. From whence came they? Only one answer can be given: They were taken from the pagans by way of compromise.

CHAPTER XIX.

THE BAPTISM OF THE SICK.

IF immersion was so universally taught in the ancient Christianity, how was sprinkling introduced? I answer in the baptism of the sick, or, as it was afterwards called, *clinic baptism*. The baptism of the sick originated in a dangerous heresy. Men had departed from the simplicity of the Gospel. The atoning efficacy of the blood of Christ was left out of sight, and the importance of baptism was overestimated. It was at this time that the doctrine of baptismal salvation was spread abroad throughout the churches. Along with it were the attendant evils, infant baptism and sprinkling. It was argued that if infants were to die unbaptized, they would be eternally condemned. Since a man upon his sick bed could not be immersed easily, and if he died unbaptized, he would be lost, it was thought that a profusion of water poured upon him might save him. This was called *clinic* baptism.

The first instance of clinic baptism upon record, indeed, the first example of affusion, is given in the Ecclesiastical History of Eusebius, which lies before me. It was the celebrated case of Novatian, A. D. 250. Eusebius says of him: "Being delivered by the exorcists, he fell into a severe sickness; and as he seemed about to die, he received baptism by affusion, on the bed where he lay; if, indeed, we can say such a one did receive it." (Nic. Fath. vol. 1, pp. 288, 289.)

I will make some reflections on this case:

1. This is the earliest instance of sprinkling upon record. Pedobaptists have searched diligently, and they have never found an earlier. When was this? Two hundred and fifty years after Christ!

2. Sprinkling had its origin in the baptism of the sick. Eusebius mentions this case as peculiar. Many writers say that sprinkling and pouring originated in the baptism of the sick. Cyprian, Bishop of Carthage, A. D. 257, in answer to Magnus, says: "You have asked also, dearest son, what I thought of those who have obtained God's grace in sickness and weakness, whether they are to be accounted legitimate Christians, for that they are not to be washed, but sprinkled, with the saving water. . . . . As far as my poor understanding conceives it, I think that the divine benefits can in no respect be mutilated and weakened; nor can any thing less occur in that case, where with full and entire faith, both of the giver

and of the receiver, is accepted what is drawn from the divine gift. . . . . In the sacrament of salvation, when necessity compels, and God bestows his mercy, the divine methods confer the whole benefit on believers; nor ought it to trouble any one that sick people seem to be sprinkled or affused when they obtain the Lord's grace." (Ante-Nic. Fath., vol. 5, pp. 400, 401.)

As late as 754 the monks of Cressy asked Pope Stephen II.: "Is it lawful, in cases of necessity occasioned by sickness, to baptize an infant by pouring water on its head from a cup or the hands?" The Pope replied: "Such a baptism, performed in such a case of necessity, shall be accounted valid." Basnage says: " This was accounted the first law against immersion."

The great historian Neander remarks: "In respect to the form of baptism, it was in conformity with the original institution and the original import of the symbol, performed by immersion, as a sign of entire baptism into the Holy Spirit, of being entirely penetrated by the same. It was only with the sick, when the exigency required it, that any exception was made; and in this case baptism was administered by sprinkling. Many superstitious persons, clinging to the outward form, imagined that such baptism by sprinkling was not fully valid; and hence they distinguished those who had been thus baptized by denominating them the *clinici.*" (Ch. Hist., vol 1, p. 310.)

Geiseler is most emphatic, and calls things by the right name. He says: "It was often necessary to baptize the sick, and in that case *sprinkling was substituted for the usual rite.*" (Ch. Hist., vol. 1, p. 159.)

3. As it has been already intimated, all persons did not hold that this baptism was valid. None thought it so good as immersion. Eusebius adds: "If, indeed, it be proper to say that one like him did receive baptism." There would have been no dispute if sprinkling had been regarded as baptism.

The historians are unanimous on this point. Dr. George C. Knapp, late Professor of Theology in the University of Halle, says: "Immersion is peculiarly agreeable to the institution of Christ, and to the practice of the apostolic church, and so even John baptized, and immersion remained common for a long time after; except that in the third century, or perhaps earlier, the baptism of the sick was performed by sprinkling or affusion. Still some would not acknowledge this to be true baptism, and controversy arose concerning it, so unheard of was it at that time to baptize by affusion." (**Knapp's Theol.,** p. 486.)

Venema testifies: "To the essential rite of baptism in the third century, pertained immersion, and not aspersion, except in cases of necessity, and it was accounted a half perfect baptism.

Salmasius: "Thus, Novatian, when sick, received baptism, being sprinkled, not baptized."

Valesius says: "Therefore, baptism of this kind was not customary, and was esteemed imperfect."

Baronius, the great Catholic historian, adds: "Those who were baptized upon their beds were *not called Christians,* but clinics." (Annals, vol. 1, p. 208, ed. 1623.)

Look at what these historians say; the introduction of sprinkling, even for the sick, caused a controversy that lasted for centuries. It was an unheard of thing. It was called a half perfect baptism, and the persons thus baptized were not called Christians, but clinics.

4. The clinics were not admitted to sacred orders. Eusebius quotes Fabius with approbation, as follows: "For this illustrious man forsook the Church of God, in which when he believed, he was judged worthy of the presbyterate through the favor of the bishop who ordained him to the presbyterial office. This had been resisted by all the

clergy and many of the laity; because it was unlawful that one who had been affused on his bed, an account of sickness, as he had been, should enter into any clerical office; but the bishop requested that he might be permitted to ordain this one only." (Nic. Fath., vol. 1, p. 289.)

This establishes the point.

Was it against the condition of Novatian being sick, or against the act of baptism that the objection was urged? I answer, against both. 1. Against the person sick. The Council of Neo-Cæsarea, in its twelfth canon, affirms: "He that is baptized when he is sick, ought not to be made a priest; for his coming to faith is not voluntary, but from necessity." 2. Against his baptism. While Novatian was living Magnus asked Cyprian, "Whether they are to be esteemed right Christians who are not washed in water but only sprinkled?" Cyprian answered, "Necessity compelling, and God granting his indulgence." Valesius says: "In addition, since baptism properly signifies immersion, a pouring of this sort could hardly be called a baptism. Wherefore clinics were forbidden to be promoted to the rank of the presbytery, by the twelfth canon of the Council of Neo-Cæsarea."

This, then, is the origin of sprinkling. From

this clinic baptism sprinkling has finally prevailed in the West among Catholics, with the exception of Milan, which still holds to immersion, and among Protestants with the exception of the Baptists. This small beginning has led to great results. "It shows how closely we should watch innovations, and how earnestly we should hold to the practice of the Scriptures. This ordinance of God's house has been changed, and so changed as to completely destroy its symbolical import. It shows how the spirit that lives and moves in human society can override the most sacred ordinances." Or, as Dean Stanley has said in another place: "These are the outward forms of which, in the Western churches, almost every particular is altered, even the most material points. Immersion has become the exception and not the rule. Adult baptism as well as immersion, exists only among the Baptists. *The dramatic action of the scene is lost.*"

CHAPTER XX.

THE HISTORY OF SPRINKLING.

IT has already been shown that sprinkling originated in the baptism of the sick. This, however, was of very doubtful authority and did not come into current use. It proved not to be popular, but was an innovation that was most generally condemned. Upon the origin of sprinkling for baptism the learned Sir David Brewster says: "It is impossible to mark the period when sprinkling was introduced. It is probable, however, that it was invented in Africa, in the second century, in favor of clinics. But it was so far from being approved of the church in general, that the Africans themselves did not count it valid." (Edin. Ency., vol. 3, p. 236.)

Before the Reformation sprinkling made very indifferent headway. Now and then it had an advocate, but it did not prevail. All of the reformers recognized immersion as the primitive act of baptism. They had no hesitation in freely expressing themselves. Luther, in his work on *The Sacrament of Baptism*, says: "First, baptism is a Greek word. In Latin it can be translated *immersion*, as when we plunge something into water, that it may be completely covered with water; and although that custom has been given up by most persons—for they do not wholly submerge the children, but only pour on them a little water, yet they ought to have been completely immersed and straightway drawn out again."

Luther voiced the opinion of all of the reformers, but the popish practice of sprinkling had already set in and the tide was too great to be resisted. The Greeks, not being under the authority of the Pope, would not give way and so practice immersion till this day. But in other quarters sprinkling became well nigh universal.

The question then naturally comes up, from whence came this sprinkling. That it was a change in the original act there can be no doubt. "The question now arises," says Dr. Schaff, the eminent Presbyterian scholar, "when and how came the mode of pouring and sprinkling to take the place of immersion and emersion, as a rule. The *change* was gradual and confined to the Western churches. The Roman Church, as we have seen, backed by the authority of Thomas Aquinas, 'the Angelic Doctor,' took the lead in the thirteenth century, yet so as to retain in her rituals the form of immersion as the older and better mode. The practice prevailed over theory, and the exception became the rule." (Teach. p. 51.)

France appears to have been the first country where sprinkling prevailed. That country was more completely under the power and spirit of the Pope than any other, and it at once accepted the doctrine that the Church had a right to change any ordinance at its will. Says Dr. Wall: "France seems to have been the first country in the world where baptism by affusion was used ordinarily to persons in health, and in the public way of administering it. . . . From France it spread (but not till a good while after) into Italy, Germany, Spain, &c., and last of all into England." (Hist. In. Bap. vol. 1, p. 576, 577.)

Sir David Brewster gives such a clear account of the origin of sprinkling that I present what he says in this connection. Says he: "The first law for sprinkling was obtained in the following manner: Pope Stephen III. being driven from Rome by Astulphus, king of the Lombards, in 753, fled to Pepin, who, a short time before, had usurped the crown of France. Whilst he remained there, the Monks of Cressy in Brittany consulted him, whether, in a case of necessity, baptism, performed by pouring water on the head of the infant, would be lawful. Stephen replied, that it would. But though the truth of this fact should be allowed, which some Catholics deny, yet pouring or sprinkling was only admitted in cases of necessity. It was not till 1311, that the legislature, in a Council held at Ravenna, declared immersion or sprinkling to be indifferent." (Edinburg Ency. vol. 3, p. 236.)

But it is a remarkable fact that the cold countries held on to immersion longer than the warm countries. France, a southern country, introduced sprinkling; but England, a cold country, held on to immersion. It was not until the time of bloody Mary that sprinkling was introduced into England. Dr. Wall says: "One would have thought that the cold countries should have been the first that should have changed the custom from dipping to affusion, because in cold climates the bathing of the body in water may seem much more unnatural and dangerous to the health than in the hot ones (and it is to be noted, by the way, that all of those countries of whose rites of baptism, and immersion used in it, we have any account in the Scriptures or other ancient history, are in hot climates, where frequent and common bathing both of infants and grown persons is natural, and even necessary to the health). But by history it appears that the cold climates held the custom of dipping as long as any; for England, which is one of the coldest, was one of the latest that admitted this *alteration* of the ordinary way." (Wall's Hist. vol. 1, p. 575.)

As to just how universal dipping was in England at this period I will let Dr. Schaff relate: "King Edward VI.," says he, "and Queen Elizabeth were immersed. The first Prayer Book of Edward VI. (1549), followed the Office of Sarum, directs the priest to dip the child in water thrice: 'first, dypping the right side; secondly, the left side; the third time, dypping the face toward the fonte.' In the second Prayer Book (1552) the priest is simply directed to dip the child discreetly and warily; and permission is given, for the first time in Great Britain, to substitute pouring if the godfathers and godmothers certify that the child is weak. 'During the reign of Elizabeth,' says Dr. Wall, 'many fond ladies and gentlewomen first, and then by degrees the common people, would obtain the favor of the priests to have their children pass for weak children too tender to endure dipping in the water.' The same writer traces the practice of sprinkling to the period of the Long Parliament and the Westminster Assembly. 'This *change* in England and other Protestant countries from immersion to pouring, and from pouring to sprinkling, was encouraged by the authority of Calvin, who declared the mode to be a matter of no importance; and by the

Westminster Assembly of Divines (1643–1652), which decided that pouring and sprinkling are 'not only lawful, but also sufficient.' The Westminster Confession declares: 'Dipping of the person into the water is not necessary; but baptism is rightly administered by pouring or sprinkling water upon the person.'" (Teach. pp. 51, 52.)

It was largely through the authority of Calvin that sprinkling came into general use in England. I am anxious to have these statements historically correct, and therefore I give them in the words of others. Sir David Brewster, whom I have so often quoted in this chapter, is unquestioned authority. His account is as follows: "During the persecution of Mary, many persons, most of whom were Scotchmen, fled from England to Geneva, and there greedily imbibed the opinions of that church. In 1556 a book was published in that place containing 'The Form of Prayer and Ministration of the Sacraments, approved by the famous and godly learned man, John Calvin,' in which the administrator is enjoined to take water in his hand and lay it upon the child's forehead. These Scotch exiles, who had renounced the authority of the Pope, implicitly acknowledged the authority of Calvin; and returning to their own country, with Knox at their head, in 1559, established sprinkling in Scotland. From Scotland this practice made its way into England in the reign of Elizabeth, but was not authorized by the established church. In the Assembly of Divines, held at Westminster in 1643, it was keenly debated whether immersion or sprinkling should be adopted: 25 voted for sprinkling, and 24 for immersion; and even this small majority was obtained at the earnest request of Dr. Lightfoot, who had acquired great influence in that Assembly. Sprinkling is therefore the general practice of this country. Many Christians, however, especially the Baptists, reject it. The Greek Church universally adheres to immersion." (Edin. Ency. vol. 3, p. 236.)

The account of this change as given by Dean Stanley, the English High-Church Episcopalian, is intensely entertaining. He says: "We now pass to the *changes* in the form itself. For the first thirteen centuries the almost universal practice of baptism was that of which we read in the New Testament, and which is the very meaning of the word baptize: that those who were baptized were plunged, submerged, immersed into the water. That practice is still, as we have seen, continued in Eastern churches. In the Western Church it still lingers among Roman Catholics in the solitary instance of the Cathedral of Milan; amongst Protestants in the numerous sect of the Baptists. It lasted long into the Middle Ages. Even the Icelanders, who at first shrank from the water of their freezing lakes, were reconciled when they found that they could use the warm water of the Geysers. And the cold climate of Russia has not been found an obstacle to its continuance throughout that vast empire. Even in the Church of England it is still observed in theory. The Rubric in the public baptism for infants enjoins that, unless for special causes, they are to be dipped, not sprinkled. Edward VI. and Elizabeth were both immersed. But since the beginning of the seventeenth century the practice has become exceedingly rare. With the few exceptions just mentioned, the whole of the Western churches have now *substituted* for the ancient bath the ceremony of letting fall a few drops of water on the face." (Institutes, pp. 18, 19.)

These historical statements prove beyond doubt that sprinkling is of a popish origin. Where the Pope of Rome has not had control, sprinkling has never been practiced. This is a notorious fact, and is worthy of serious consideration. Dr. Wall, and he was a staunch Episcopalian, makes this plain enough. Says he: "Sprinkling, for the common use of baptizing, was really introduced (in France first, and then in the other *popish countries*) *in times of popery;* and that accordingly all those countries in which the usurped power of the Pope is or has been owned have left off dipping of children in the font; but that *all other countries in the world (which have never regarded his authority)* do still use it; and that basins, except that in case of necessity, were never used by papist or any other Christians whatsoever till by themselves." (Wall's Hist. p. 583.)

Here are the plainest and most emphatic declarations of Pedobaptist scholars that immersion was changed to sprinkling, and this by the authority of Rome. Sprinkling, then, does not come from the New Testament, but from the Roman Catholic Church. It also teaches the dangerous tendency of innovations. Beginning with the affusion of a sick man, it has overthrown the entire act as commanded by Christ, and substituted an entirely different thing in its place. The beauty and symbolism of the ordinance have been destroyed. As for our part, let us abide by the plain teaching of God's word, and we are not likely to go astray.

CHAPTER XXI.

WHAT THE COUNCILS OF THE ROMAN CATHOLIC CHURCH SAY.

FROM early times until now it has been the custom of the Roman Catholic Church to call together councils concerning the welfare of that church. Some of those that I shall notice are called General Councils, representing the general interest of that church; while others were Provincial, representing only limited sections. The authorities I present are unquestioned. Labbe and Cossart's edition of the Councils is a very elaborate work, and is of indisputable authority. This immense work is by two Jesuits, and nothing contrary to Catholic faith is likely to be found in its pages. It is in seventeen large Latin volumes, and bears date, Paris, 1671. The other references are equally authoritative, though not so extensive.

The acts of the first General Nicene Council, A. D. 325, are in favor of immersion. The following is found in the acts of the Council: "He who is baptized descends indeed, obnoxious to sins, and held with the corruptions of slavery; but he ascends, free from the slavery and sins, a son of

God, heir—yea, co-heir—with Christ, having put on Christ, as it is written, 'As many of you as were baptized into Christ have put on Christ.'"

In the Council of Carthage, A. D. 348, there was a fierce discussion of the subject of baptism. Several bishops spoke, and their speeches have been preserved. Bishop Gratus said: "I ask this sacred assembly to express their opinion whether, after a man has descended into the water, and has been questioned as to his belief in the Trinity, according to the faith of the Gospel and the doctrines of the Apostles, and has made a good confession concerning the resurrection of Jesus Christ, he ought to be again questioned concerning the same faith, and again immersed in water?" All the bishops answered, "Far be it, far be it." (Labbe and Cos. vol. 2, p. 1821.)

In 633 the Spanish Council known as the Fourth Council of Toledo was called by King Sisimand. It was composed of the Archbishops of Seville, Narbonne, Braga, Merida, Toledo, and Tarragona, with fifty-three suffragan bishops, and with seven presbyters representing bishops. A change had been made from trine to single immersion. Although this change had been indorsed by the most venerable bishops, and by a letter from Pope Gregory, the people were indignant and much excited.

To calm this excitement and unite the Spanish Catholics this Council decreed: "For shunning the schism or the use of an heretical practice, we observe a single immersion in baptism. Nor do they who immerse three times appear to us to approve of the claim of heretics, although they follow their custom (of trine immersion). And that no one may doubt the propriety of this single sacrament, let him see that it is the death and resurrection of Christ shown forth. For the immersion in the waters is a descent, as it were, into the grave; and, again, the emersion from the waters is a resurrection. Likewise he may see displayed in it the unity of the Deity and the Trinity of persons—the unity whilst we immerse once, and the Trinity whilst we baptize in the name of the Father, and of the Son, and of the Holy Ghost." (Labbe and Cos. vol. 1, pp. 1705, 1706.) The Council first of all indorsed the letter of Gregory, which became famous, and has been quoted in all controversies since, and then passed this decree in favor of single immersion.

In 787 the Council of Calcuith, in England, sent an account of its enactments to Pope Adrian I. by Gregory and Theophylact, and, among other things, they stated that baptism was to be performed in the font on the festivals of Easter and Whitsuntide.

The following are the recommendations of the second canon: "That baptism be performed according to the canons, and not at any other time except in cases of emergency; and that all who receive children from the holy font, and answer for those who can not speak for the renouncing of Satan and his works and pomps, and for believing the faith, know that they are their sureties unto the Lord according to their promise; and when they shall have attained to a competent age, let them teach the aforesaid Lord's prayer and creed." (Hart's Eccl. Rec. p. 195.)

The second council of Calcuith was held in the kingdom of Mercia in 816, and was presided over by Mulfud, Archbishop of Canterbury. The eleventh canon insists on immersion in these strong words: "Let presbyters also know that when they administer baptism they ought not to pour the consecrated water upon the infants' heads, but let them always be immersed in the font; as the Son of God himself afforded an example unto all believers when he was three times immersed in the river Jordan." (Hart's Eccl. Rec. p. 195.) The learned Collier said of this canon that, "by enjoining the priest not to sprinkle the infants in baptism shows the great regard they had for the primitive usage of immersion; that they did not look upon this as a dangerous rite, or at all impractical in these northern climates; not that they thought this circumstance essential to the sacrament, but because it was the general practice of the primitive church; because it was a lively, instructive emblem of the death, burial, and resurrection of our Saviour; for this reason they preferred it to sprinkling." (Collier's Eccl. Hist. vol. 1, p. 354.) This is a very practical admission, coming as it does from the leading historian of the Episcopal Church of England. To the fact that this Council decreed immersion, and repudiated sprinkling, this historian is a very competent witness, but as to the reason why this was done we have as much right to an opinion as he had. They decreed immersion because it was the apostolic rite.

The Council of Worms, A. D. 868, passed a decree almost identically like that of the Council of Toledo given above, and the reason was the same: "While some priests baptized with three immersions, and the others with but one, a schism was raised, endangering the unity of the Church." (Can. 5.)

The Council of Tribur, A. D. 895, makes use of these strong words: "Trine immersion is an imitation of the three days' burial, and the rising again out of the water is an image of Christ rising from the grave." (Labbe and Cos., vol. 9, p. 446.)

The Council of Cashel, under Henry II., A. D. 1172, was called to secure uniformity between the English and Irish churches. Canon 1 reads: "That children be brought to the church and be baptized there in pure water, with a threefold immersion; and that this be done by priests, unless when there is imminent danger of death, when it may be administered by any one without distinction of sex or order." (Hart's Eccl. Rec., p. 202.)

Another Council held at Cashel about the same time decreed: "That infants be catechised before the doors of the church, and then be baptized in the font, in baptismal churches." (Hart's Eccl. Rec., p. 202.)

The Council of York, 1185, also decreed in favor of immersion.

The Westminster General Council, held in London, A. D. 1200, decreed: "If a layman baptize a child in case of necessity, let all that follows after the immersion, (the chrism, etc.) be performed by a priest." (Can. 3.)

The Council of Worcester, 1240, speaks of immersion in these words: "We enjoin that in every church where baptism is performed, there shall be a font of stone of sufficient size and depth for the baptizing of children, and it shall be deeply covered, ... such little candidate for baptism be thrice immersed." And a further decree: "But children baptized in case of necessity, if they recover, must be brought to the church, that those things that are wanting may be supplied, namely—those things which follow the immersion in baptism."

The Council of Clermont, A. D. 1268, considering a baptism that had been performed by a layman in case of necessity, decreed: "At the font every thing which is usually done shall be performed, the immersion only excepted, but if it is doubtful under what form of words the child has been baptized, then let the priest baptize him; but while he immerses him, let him say, "If thou art not already baptized, I baptize thee in the name of the Father," etc.

The Council of Reading, 1279, decreed that the children should be baptized only at Easter and Pentecost, cases of necessity excepted; and that in the meantime they should be instructed, "so that immersion alone remains to be performed on the day of baptism." (Can. 4.)

The Council of Oxford, 1222, decreed: "Let not above three persons be admitted to raise the child from the holy font." (Hart's Eccl. Rec., p. 205.)

The Council of Cologne, in 1280, decreed: "That he who baptizes, when he immerses the candidate in water, shall neither add to the words, or take from them, or change them."

The Council of Nismes, 1284, decreed that: "The baptizer shall thrice immerse the infant in water, but if one immersion have been performed, the child will nevertheless be baptized." (Labbe and Cos., vol. 11, p. 1199.)

The Council of Ravenna, 1311, decreed: "Baptism is to be administered by trine aspersion or immersion." (Labbe and Cos., vol. 11, B. 2, p. 1586.)

This is the first time in history that sprinkling or immersion were made indifferent. It is well to say that this Council only represented one province. Soon after this sprinkling became customary in France, but immersion prevailed in England until the seventeenth century.

In 1355, the Council of Prague decreed: "Let the presbyters take heed lest any negligence be committed, either in putting together or in the expression of the proper form of words, as well as in the immersion in water with which the whole value of baptism is connected. As to the form, let the immersion be trine, in this manner—that at once, when the administrator begins to utter the prescribed form, he does that which is first and that which is last when he finishes."

From this time sprinkling rapidly prevailed in the Catholic Church, and has become universal with them except in the church at Milan.

CHAPTER XXII.

THE TESTIMONY OF LITURGIES AND RITUALS.

I RARELY, if ever, heard the Liturgies and Missals referred to in an argument upon the action of baptism, and yet I consider that they give very strong testimony in favor of immersion. The Roman Catholic Martini says: "In all of the pontificals and rituals I have seen, and I have seen many, ancient as well as more recent, immersion is prescribed. I must except, however, the ritual of the church of Madeleine de Beaulieu, the age of which does not exceed three hundred years, in which the priest is directed to pour water on the head of the infant." A ritual is of more weight than the testimony of any individual could be; for it represents the opinion and practice of a church, or of many churches, while an individual only expresses his own sentiments. I here present a number of these rituals:

The Gothic Missal, a very old manuscript, has the following prayer in the baptismal benediction: "We pray our Lord God that he will sanctify this font, so that all who will descend into this font may receive through the washing of the blessed laver, the remission of their sins."

The Syrian Ritual, as used by the Nestorians, appears to be decisive: "They bring them to the priest, who, standing on the western side of the baptistery, turns the child's face to the east, and immerses him in water, putting his hand on his head, and saying, such a one is baptized in the name of the Father, etc." (Badger's Nestorians and their Ritual, vol. 2, pp. 207, 208.)

The Baptismal Liturgy, which formed a part of the Sacramentary of Pope Gelasius, A. D. 492, and which was taken by Cardinal Thomasins, 1748, from a codex manuscript, more than a thousand years old, reads thus: "Then immerse three times in water."

Remingius, who baptized King Clovis, in a ritual taken from a very old manuscript, says: "The presbyters or the deacons, or, if need be, acolythis, having put on their robes, proceed to the font, and enter into the water, and receive therefrom their parents, baptize, first the males, and then the females, by trine immersion, with but one invocation of the Holy Trinity, saying: I baptize thee into the name of the Father, and dips once, and of the Son, and dips again, and of Holy Ghost, and dips the third time."

An ancient ritual found in a manuscript codex of the Monastery of Glogan, in the diocese of Cologne, says: "The presbyter receiving the infant from its parents, asking its name, first baptizes the males, and then the females, by trine immersion, saying: I baptize thee in the name, etc."

The Ordo Romanus, a Ritual of the eighth century, has: "I baptize thee in the name of the Father, (and immerses once,) and of the Son, (and immerses the second time,) and of the Holy Ghost, (and immerses the third time)."

The Manual of Sarum, drawn up about 1085, by Osmond, Bishop of Salisbury and Chancellor of England, and adopted by nearly all of England, Wales and Ireland, and continued in use till Edward the VI., has: "The priest shall take the child into his hands, and 'asking his name, baptize him by trine immersion, thus calling on the name of the Trinity, he shall say: N., I baptize thee in the name of the Father, and dips him once, etc."

This manual was regarded as very great authority. Wall quotes it and says: "The offices or liturgies for public baptism in the Church of England did all along, so far as I can learn, enjoin dipping, without any mention of pouring or sprinkling. And John Frith, writing in the year 1533, a treatise on baptism, calls the outward part of it, the plunging down into the water, and lifting up again, which he often mentions, without ever mentioning pouring or sprinkling." (Wall's Hist. Int. Bap. vol. 1, p. 579.) And Wheatly, writing on the Book of Common Prayer, in 1885, says: "The Salisbury Missal, printed in 1530, (the last that was in force before the Reformation,) expressly requires and orders dipping." (p. 350.)

In a ritual formerly belonging to the church at Ravenna, a manuscript of the twelfth century, and until lately in possession of Jos. Baptista Martini, but now in the library of the University of the city of Bologna, we find: "Then taking him, (the candidate) he baptized him, with trine immersion, saying, Wilt thou be baptized? Answer, I will, three times, And I baptize thee in the name of the Father, and dips him once, etc."

Guillaume Durant, Bishop of Mendefurn, 1286–1296, prescribed a ritual for his clergy, in which the following passage occurs: "That he who baptizes, after giving a name to the child, and made the sign of the cross upon the water, must plunge the infant three times, ... he shall immerse the child."

M. De Moleon alludes to an ancient ritual of

the year 1581, which prescribes immersion: "The presbyter shall say to the boy, I baptize thee into the name of the Father, immerse once, etc."

The first prayer book of Edward VI. reads: "First, dipping the right side; secondly, the left side; third time dipping the face toward the font." The second prayer book of Edward, 1551, the first book of Queen Elizabeth, 1559, and that of King James, in 1604, all read: "The priest shall dip him in the water, discreetly and warily; but if they certify that the child is weak, it shall suffice to pour water upon it." This book of Edward is the first authentic permission for altering the act of baptism in Great Britain, yet Dean Stanley asserts that "Edward the VI. and Elizabeth were both immersed." (Christian Institutions, p. 18.)

The Saxon Visitation Articles, 1592, Art. iii, says: "That there is but one baptism, and one ablution: not that which is used to take away the filth of the body, but that which washes us from our sins. By baptism, as the bath of regeneration and renovation of the Holy Ghost, God saves us, and works in us such justice and purgation from our sins, etc." (Schaff's Creeds of Christendom, vol. 3, p. 184.)

The order of the Sacraments, prepared by Pope Gregory I., in 1776, has: "Let the priest baptize with a trine immersion, once only invoking the Trinity.'"

The Methodist Discipline, so late as 1846, asserted that Christ was baptized "in the river of Jordan," and that "buried in baptism" alludes to water baptism.

The present Ritual of the Greek Church reads: "And when the whole body is anointed, the priest immerses him, holding him erect, and looking toward the east, saying, the servant of the God is immersed, in the name of the Father, and of the Son, and of the Holy Spirit; now and ever, and to ages of ages, amen. At each invocation, bringing him down, and bringing him up. And after the immersing, the priest washes his hands, singing with the people: Happy they, whose sins are forgiven, etc."

I only ask that you shall weigh the evidence here submitted. These rituals represent, or have represented, much of the faith and practice of the world.

CHAPTER XXIII.

WHAT THE POETS SAY.

PAUL, in the sermon which he delivered at Athens, thought it legitimate to appeal to their own poets. I will also refer to this class of writers. I have long observed that all of the principal poets have favored immersion as the rite of Christian baptism, but for some reason they are not often quoted. The evidence I introduce is of two kinds: 1st, a direct statement to this effect; and, 2nd, an illustration of the classical use of the word. I will give what several of the poets have to say on the subject.

Dante, A. D. 1300, in his vision of hell, describes some apertures in the rocks of torment, of the same dimensions as the fonts of St. John the Baptist at Florence:

> "I saw the livid stone throughout the sides,
> And its bottom full of apertures,
> All equal in their width, and circular each;
> Nor ample less nor larger they appear'd
> Than in Saint John's fair dome of me belov'd,
> Those fram'd to hold the pure baptismal streams,
> One of the which I brake, some few years past,
> To save a whelming infant; and be this
> A seal to undeceive whoever doubts

The motive of my deed. From out the mouth
Of every one emerg'd a sinner's feet,
And of the legs high upward as the calf;
The rest beneath was hid."

There is a passage in Dante that throws light on the much quoted words of Polybius: "The foot-soldiers were baptized as far as the breast." Lately some have contended that immerse was not a proper rendering of baptize in this passage. The poet says of some of the lost in hell:

"In the pit they stand immers'd,
Each from his navel downward."

The bard believed in baptismal salvation by immersion, and hence he makes Beatrice exhort Christians:

"Be ye more staid,
O Christians; not, like feather, by each wind
Removable; nor think to cleanse yourselves
In every water."

He says of himself:

"I return'd
From the most holy wave, regenerate,
E'en as new plants renew'd with foliage new,
Pure and made apt for mounting the stars."

The Vision of Pierce Plowman, of the fourteenth century, has the following:

"Trojanus was a true knight, and toke never Christendom,
And he is safe, sayeth the boke, and his soule in heaven;
For there is fulling in fonte, and fulling in blud sheding,
And through fire is fullynge, that is firm believe."

This style of writing was common before the Reformation. Baptism is here called fulled, which was performed in a baptistery, and of course by immersion. The following is from the same work:

"Quod he,
May no medicine on mold the man to heal brynge,
Neither faith ne sine hope, so festered he hys wounds,
Wythout the bloud of a barne bore of a mayden,
And he bathed in that blood baptized as it were
Than plastered with penance, and passion of that baby,
He should stand and step, and stalworth he never
Till he have eaten all the barne, and his bloud drunken."

The celebrated **Lodovico Ariosto**, who composed his Orlando Furioso A. D. 1504, understood baptism as a dipping. Of one of his heroes he says:

"On the portentious bridge he meant to meet
   Whatever champion dar'd the pass to try,
And send the warrior and his steed to fleet
   Down the deep flood that swept his castle by.
. . . .
   His falling foe the Algerine compell'd
To quaff at large the cool and temp'rate flood,
   For that Circean draught that late impell'd
His cruel hand to shed a virgin's blood,
As if that *baptismal rite* could ease his inward load.
Fool, to suppose that the surge could wash away
   The bloody orgies of the venom'd bowl;
Yet many a knight who fought the dubious fray
By turns were sent adown the flood to roll."

Pollok, in speaking of the loss of freedom, says of some who defended slavery:

> "Of Christian parentage descended, too,
>   And dipped in the baptismal font, as sign
>   Of dedication to the Prince who bowed
>   To death, to set the sin-bound prisoner free."

The pious Isaac Watts sings:

> "Do we not know that solemn word,
>   That we are buried with the Lord?
>   Baptized into his death, and then
>   Put off the body of our sin."

Cowper in his Task says of Philosophy:

> "Philosophy baptiz'd
> In the pure fountain of eternal love,
>   Has eyes indeed."

And who has not sung the words of this poet:

> "There is a fountain filled with blood
>   Drawn from Immanuel's veins;
>   And sinners, plunged beneath that flood,
>   Lose all their guilty stains."

This plunging in the blood of Christ has a fit emblem in buried with Christ in baptism.

The classical expression "baptized in sleep" is well explained by Cowper:

> "Immersed in soft repose ambrosial."

Virgil sings of the Greeks taking Troy:

> "They invade the city buried in sleep and wine."

Pope in his Odyssey translates the root of baptize to plunge. When the eyes of Polyphemus are bored out with a red-hot iron, he compares it with a smith tempering his steel:

> "As when armourers temper in the ford
> The keen edge pole-axe, or the shining sword,
> The red-hot metal hisses in the lake,
> Thus in the eye-ball hissed the plunging stake."

Pope thus relates the death of one of Homer's heroes:

> "Plunged in his throat the smoking weapon lies."

Mr. Dryden likewise expresses the poet's sense thus in the Æneid:

> "Thus having said, her smould'ring torch unpress'd,
> With her full force she plunged into his breast."

Aratus, describing the setting of the constellation Cepheus in latitude sixty-nine or seventy degrees, calls it baptizing or plunging his upper parts into the sea; and, "also if the sun baptizes himself without a cloud into the western sea." These expressions are often found in the poets. Virgil, as translated by Dryden, in speaking of the Greater and Lesser Bears, says they—

> "By fate's decree
> Abhor to dive beneath the northern sea."

Homer tells of a hero who was—

> "Like the red star that fires the autumnal skies,
> When fresh he rears his radiant orb to sight,
> And bath'd in ocean shoots a keener light."

And Bickersteth says:
"The sun,
Who climbing the meridian steep of heaven,
Shone with a monarch's glory, till he dipp'd
His footsteps in the ruddy western waves."

And again:

"It was golden eventide. The sun
Was sinking through the roseate clouds to rest
Beneath the western waves."

Bickersteth in that beautiful poem, "Yesterday, To-day, and Forever," speaks thus of the work of the Baptist:
"Jerusalem
Hurried to Jordan. 'Ah, what deeds of wrong
Lips, counted by their fellows as pure as babes,
Flung then upon startled winds! What filth
Was wash'd away from penitential hearts
In that baptismal stream.'"

Of the baptism of Jesus he says:
"John, abash'd,
Shrank from the suit he urged. But he refused
Refusal. And, as from the shallow ford
Returning, on the bank he knelt in prayer."

The poet also throws light on the much disputed passage, Rev. xix: 13: "And he was clothed in a vesture dipped in blood." He says:
"Who knows not
The loves of David and young Jonathan,
When in unwitting rivalry of hearts
The son of Jesse won a nobler wreath
Than garlands pluck'd in war and dipp'd in blood."

In another passage he expressly refers to this passage:

> "The Lord of hosts,
> Apparell'd in a vesture dipp'd in blood."

John the Baptist said that Christ, when he came, would baptize the wicked in the fires of hell. Bickersteth in the "Millennial Sabbath" catches the spirit of this when he describes how God utterly ruined some of the fallen angels:

> "He hurled them down
> Like meteors through the lurid vault, **and fix'd**
> Their adamantine fetters to a rock
> Of adamant, submerged, not consumed,
> Beneath the lake of fire."

And the wicked sank—

> "Still down, still ever down, from deep to deep,
> Into the outer darkness, till at last
> The fiery gulf received them, and they **plunged**
> **Beneath Gehennah's sulphureous waves**
> In the abyss of ever enduring woe."

This poet also gives us a significant **exposition** of the "baptism of suffering":

> "The Sun
> Of Righteousness, with healing in his wings,
> Has risen upon a world weary of night:
> Most glorious, when emergent from the flood
> That from far Lebanon to Kadesh roll'd
> Its waves of fire baptismal, Zion rose
> In perfect beauty."

Moore, ever popular with many, adds his testimony. Julian, in his ode to Cupid, says he caught the boy, baptized him in wine, and drank him. Moore thus sings of this event:

> "I caught him by his downy wing,
> And whelm'd him in the racy spring:
> Ah, then I drank the poison'd bowl,
> And love now nestles in my soul."

The classic "baptized in wine" is explained by Moore. He says of wine, personified as Bacchus, that—

> "To my inmost love he glides,
> And bathes it with his ruby tides."

I now refer to the immortal Milton. The Archangel Michael is explaining to Adam the plan of salvation, and finally tells him of the great commission, when he says:

> "Them who shall believe,
> Baptizing in the profluent stream, the sign
> Of washing them from guilt of sin to life
> Pure, and in mind prepar'd, if so befall,
> For death, like that which the Redeemer died."

The last quotation is from Paradise Lost; this one is from Paradise Regained. Satan sees the thousands coming to the baptism of John, and in alarm he speaks of Christ to his hosts:

> "Before Him a great prophet, to proclaim
> His coming, is sent Harbinger, who all

> Invites, and in the consecrated stream
> Pretends to wash off sin, and fit them so
> Purified to receive Him pure, or rather
> To do Him honor as their king; all come,
> And he himself among them was baptized;
> Not thence to be more pure, but to receive
> The testimony of heaven, that who He is
> Thenceforth the nations may not doubt. I saw
> The prophet do him reverence, on Him rising
> Out of the water, heaven above the clouds
> Unfold her crystal doors, thence on His head
> A perfect dove descends, whate'er it meant."

Christ, while meditating in the wilderness, speaks of this transaction:

> (The Baptist)—"first
> Refused on me his baptism to confer,
> As much his greater, and was hardly won;
> But as I rose out of the laving stream
> Heaven open'ed her eternal doors."

Among the Greeks *bapto* was used with the signification "to dye," because dyeing was done by dipping. So Milton has used it in his beautiful description of the angel Raphael:

> "The middle pair of his wings
> Girt like a starry zone his waist, and round
> Skirted his loins and thighs with downy gold
> And colors dipped in heaven."

Bickersteth has the same idea:

> "The stones
> Of purest crystal are from gloomiest mines;
> The tenderest pearls are won from roughest seas;

> And stars of colors dipp'd in Iris' vats
> Beam from unfathomable distances
> Ere they disclose their radiance."

I might add other names and extracts, but these are sufficient.

CHAPTER XXIV.

WHAT THE GREEK CHURCH SAYS.

I HAVE shown in former chapters that *baptizo* in classic Greek, in the Septuagint, in the New Testament, and in the Greek fathers, means to dip. The Greek Church practices dipping to-day, and has never held to any other form of baptism. I present the practice of the Greek Church as an unanswerable argument in faver of immersion. We will consider:

1. Ancient and modern Greek is substantially the same language in structure and in words. In twenty-five hundred years there has been but little variation in this language. This point alone is enough to put the whole baptismal controversy at rest.

Upon the harmony of ancient and modern Greek I give the testimony of two among the foremost teachers of Greek in this country, and what they state is confirmed by scholars in Germany, England and America.

Prof. A. F. Fleet, LL. D., for many years professor of Greek in the State University of Missouri,

WHAT THE GREEK CHURCH SAYS. 193

and who spent much time in Athens in the study of this language, writes me:

MEXICO, Mo., Jan. 26th, 1891.

REV. J. T. CHRISTIAN, *Jackson, Miss.*:

Dear Sir,—In answer to yours of the 17th inst., I would say that the modern Greek language is substantially the same in structure and in words as that spoken and written by the ancient Greeks. As I have frequently said in public and in private, Socrates and Plato, Xenophon and Demosthenes, and even Homer himself, might to-day sit at the foot of the Acropolis and read the morning paper published in Athens with comparatively little difficulty. There has been less change in the Greek language within the past 2,300 years than in the English within the past 500.

With regards, I am, very truly,

A. F. FLEET.

Prof. Addison Hogue, Professor of Greek in the University of Mississippi, and author of a learned work on Attic Prose, writes:

OXFORD, MISS., Jan. 21st, 1891.

REV. J. T. CHRISTIAN, D. D.:

My Dear Sir,—Yours of the 17th is post marked the 20th, and was received by me this morning, which will explain what might seem a tardiness in replying.

My answer is, modern Greek *is* substantially the same as the old Greek: it is far more like the Greek of 2,200 years ago than modern English is like the English of 500 years ago. English has taken in numerous words from outside languages; modern Greek has naturally a great many Turkish words; and the language as spoken among the *uneducated* people, and the colloquial Romaic, has departed very widely from the old classical standard. But the written language is amazingly like what Greek used to be. A modern Greek newspaper is easy to read, provided one can read ancient Greek with ease. Children's school books show the same similarity; and the foreign words of which I spoke are by no means so numerous as might be supposed.

If Xenophon were handed in the "Islands of the Blessed," the paper I send you, it would give him the least trouble in the world to read it, though he would naturally wonder who had been tampering with his good old Greek. You may use this as you like.

Command me further if I can be of service.

Yours, very truly,   ADDISON HOGUE.

WHAT THE GREEK CHURCH SAYS. 195

Having sufficiently emphasized the fact that ancient and modern Greek is the same language, I now pass to the proof that the Greek Church now practices immersion.

2. The use of the language. I mean by use the common, every-day acceptation of words. The word baptize is in constant use among the Greeks. A modern Greek writer on natural philosophy repeatedly employs the word. In explaining the method of determining specific gravity, he says we first weigh the body, then immerse it in water, and then weigh it, thus suspended by a cord. The *Minerva,* an Athenian newspaper, in explaining the explosive gun-cotton which caused such a noise in the world thirty years ago, says: "Common cotton, well cleansed, is taken, which, being immersed (*baptizemenon*) for about half a minute in strong nitric acid, &c." Cereas, the most learned of modern Greek writers, says: "Righteousness forbids a man to dip, (baptize in) his pen in the filth of flattery." The *Age,* another Athenian newspaper, says: "The Papists verily believe that they are being saved by sprinkling (*rantizomenoi*), and not by being baptized (*baptizomenoi*)."

3. The ritual and catechism of the Greek Church. The best way to tell what a church practices, is to study their ritual and catechism;

and I propose to let the ritual and catechism of the Greek Church speak for itself: "The servant (handmaid) of God, N., is baptized in the name of the Father, amen; and of the Son, amen; and of the holy Ghost, amen; now and ever, and to ages of ages. At each invocation he immerses the candidate and raises him again." (Offic. Orien. Ch. p. 94.) And hence the Russian catechism reads: "This they hold to be a point *necessary*, that no part of the child be undipped in water."

4. The Lexicons. Prof. Sophocles, a native Greek, who long ably filled the chair of Greek in Harvard University, published a lexicon of the Roman and Byzantine periods, "extending from B. C. 140 to A. D. 1100." He defines baptize "to dip, to immerse, to sink." On the New Testament meaning of the word, he remarks: "There is no evidence that Luke and Paul, and other writers of the New Testament, put upon this verb meanings not recognized by the Greeks."

In a French and Greek lexicon, published in Athens, in 1842, the French word immerse is defined by three Greek words, *embapsis, baptisis, katadusis,* "dip in, dip, sink under."

In an English-Greek lexicon, published in Cerfee, in 1827, the word "immerge" is translated by "baptize." This was done by a zealous defender of infant sprinkling.

5. The testimony of native Greeks. The Greeks certainly ought to know what their own language teaches, and has always taught. They are unanimous in their verdict, that baptize means to immerse. I will give the testimony of a few distinguished Greeks:

The Bishop of Cyclades says: "The word baptize, explained, means a veritable dipping, and, in fact, a perfect dipping. An object is baptized when it is completely covered. This is a proper explanation of the word *baptizo*."

Bishop Platon, of Moscow, Pres. State of Greek Ch., Edinburg, 1814, says: "The Greeks and Russians always use the trine immersion."

Alex. de Stourdza, Russian State Counselor, says: "The Church of the West has, then, departed from the example of Jesus Christ; and has obliterated the whole sublimity of the exterior sign; in short, she commits an awful abuse of words and of ideas in practicing baptism by aspersion, the very term being, in itself, a derisive contradiction. The verb baptize, *immergo*, has, in fact, but one sole acceptation. It signifies, literally and always, to plunge. Baptism and immersion are, therefore, identical, and to say baptism by aspersion is as if one should say, immersion by aspersion, or any other absurdity of the same nature." (Con. sur LaDoc. et L' Esprit. p. 87.)

Prof. Timayenis, a native Greek of the Hellenic Institute, N. Y., in a lecture at Chautauqua, in 1881, speaking of the Greek religion, said: "The Greeks baptize, of course—they baptize in the real way. The Greek word *baptizo* means nothing but immerse in the water. Baptism means nothing but immersion. In the Greek language we have a different word for sprinkling. When you put a piece of wood into the water, and cover it entirely, you baptize, you do what is expressed by the Greek word baptizo. I am ready to discuss this with any divine about the Greek word. Sprinkling is not what the Bible teaches; that is a fact that you may depend on."

The Rev. Nicholas Bjerring, of New York, in his Offices of the Oriental Church, 1884, remarks: "Baptism is celebrated sometimes in the church and sometimes in private houses, as need may be. It is always administered by dipping the infant, or adult, three times into the water." (p. 13.)

Prof. N. Bonwetsch, of Dorpat University, writes me under date of May 5th, 1890: "As far as the ceremony of the Greek-Russian Church is concerned, immersion is the only method used in baptizing,"

Dr. A. Diomedes Kyriasko, of the University of Athens, Greece, writes to Rev. C. G. Jones, of Lynchburg, Va., as follows:

ATHENS, Aug., 1890.

Dear Sir,—The verb baptizo, in the Greek language, never has the meaning of to pour or to sprinkle, but invariably that of to dip. In the Greek Church, both in its earliest times and in our days, to baptize has meant to dip. It is through this process that our church baptizes, and always has baptized both infants belonging to Christian families and adults turning from any other religion to Christianity, *i. e.*, by dipping them thrice in the water. Thus also meaning by dipping, used by the Apostles, to baptize. Were it not so Paul could not have compared baptizing to the death of Christ, saying that in baptism we are buried with Christ, and arisen with him; that is to say, the old man in us has been buried, and the new man fashioned according to the likeness of Christ risen again. Since baptism, therefore, by the cleansing of the soul, this idea can only be clearly represented by the entire dipping of the body into water, and not by sprinkling or pouring. Yours truly,

DR. A. DIOMEDES KYRIASKO, *Professor*.

6. Scholars of other communions fully confirm the Greeks in this testimony. Dr. W. D. Powell, who has just returned from Athens, says in the *Western Recorder*, under date of January 8th, 1891: "One of the Professors (in the University of Athens) brought two Greek and English Lexicons, one I remember was by Dr. Sophocles, who was a Professor in Harvard University for twenty-eight years, and both lexicons rendered the word to dip, to plunge, to immerse.

"I asked the Professors what the word *baptizo* meant in Latin, and they replied, '*submergere.*' I enquired furthermore what it meant in Spanish, and they said 'immersion.'

"An intelligent Greek said: 'Don't ask me, ask any common laborer you meet on the street and he will tell you.' So when I returned to the hotel I requested the head-waiter, who was a Frenchman, to ask the porter what the word *baptizo* meant. He replied, that it meant 'to put under the water and to take out of the water.'"

The Episcopalians bear witness to the fact that the Greek Church immerses. Two witnesses are sufficient.

Dean Stanley wrote a book upon the Eastern Church, and in it he says: "There can be no question that the original form of baptism—the very meaning of the word—was complete immersion in the deep baptismal waters; and that, for at least four centuries, any other form was either unknown, or regarded in the case of dangerous illness, as an exceptional, almost a monstrous case. To this form the Eastern Church still rigidly adheres; and the most illustrious and venerable portion of it, that of the Byzantine Empire, absolutely repudiates and ignores any other mode of administration as essentially invalid." (East. Ch., p. 117.)

Dr. Wall says: "The Greek Church, in all branches of it, does still use immersion; and they hardly count a child, except in case of sickness well baptized without it. And so do all other Christians in the world, except the Latins." (Hist. Inft. Bap., vol. 1, p. 589.)

The Presbyterians give their testimony:

Dr. Schaff says: "The Oriental and the Orthodox Russian churches require even a threefold immersion, in the name of the trinity, and deny the validity of any other. They look upon the Pope of Rome as an unbaptized heretic, and would not recognize the single immersion of the Baptists. The Longer Russian Catechism thus defines baptism: 'A sacrament in which a man who believes, having his body thrice plunged in water, in the name of God, the Father, the Son, and the Holy Ghost, to a life spiritual and holy.' Marriott, (in Smith and Cheatham, i: 161) says: 'Triple immersion, that is thrice dipping the head whilst standing in the water, was the all but universal rule of the church in early times.'" (Hist. Ch. Church, vol. 1, p. 468, note.)

Prof. Moses Stuart, of Andover, says: "The mode of baptism by immersion, the Oriental Church has always continued to preserve, even down to the present time. The members of this church are accustomed to call the members of the Western churches, sprinkled Christians, by way of ridicule and contempt." (On Bapt., p. 151.)

The Methodists join in proving the same thing.

Dr. Bennett, whose work is edited and endorsed by Bishop Hurst and Dr. Crooks, says: "The Greek Church adheres to trine immersion with great tenacity, and to-day practices this mode in all its chief churches." (Arch. p. 408.)

Prof. Bonet-Maurey, of the Theological Faculty, Paris, France, writes me: "Baptism by immersion is still practiced by all the different orthodox Greek churches of the East."

I could add many other learned witnesses, but these are sufficient. They include some of the brightest lights of Europe and America. Here is the testimony of the Greek Church as given by itself, and its representative men; and the most scholarly Episcopalians, Presbyterians and Methodists confirm this view. Some of these men have only recently investigated this subject and give us overwhelming facts. Here is a church that speaks the language that the New Testament was written in, a people that have the very words that Christ selected to designate the ordinance of baptism, in constant use. Above all, they have practiced immersion since the days of Christ. This proof to a candid mind is unanswerable.

CHAPTER XXV.

WHAT THE CATHOLICS SAY.

THOMAS AQUINAS, the great Catholic Divine of the Middle Ages, who died 1274, appears to have been the first person in the Catholic Church who took the ground that affusion under ordinary circumstances would answer for baptism. Yet he did not think it so good as immersion. He also said that "by immersion the burial with Christ is more vividly represented; therefore, this is the more common and commendable way." He also declares it to be safer. His contemporary, Bonaventura, says that "the way of dipping into water is the more common, and the fitter and the safer." This opinion favoring sprinkling, however, was not endorsed by any Council or Pope. It was not till the Council of Ravenna that sprinkling was declared to be indifferent. This was the first official action of the Catholic Church.

The foremost Catholic scholars have no hesitation in declaring that the Scripture act of baptism was by immersion. I give the testimony of some unimpeachable witnesses.

Dr. Dollinger, of Bonn University, who recently

died at a ripe old age, says: "At first Christian baptism commonly took place in the Jordan; of course, as the church spread more widely, also in private houses. Like that of St. John, it was by immersion of the whole person, which is the only meaning of the New Testament word. A mere pouring or sprinkling was never thought of." (First Age of Christ and Ch. p. 318.) He also says in his Church History, vol. 2, p. 294: "Baptism was administered by an entire immersion in water."

Arnoldi says: "*Baptizein, to immerse, to submerge.* It was as being an entire submersion under the water, since washings were already a confession of impurity and a symbol of purification—the confession of entire impurity and a symbol of entire purification." (Com. on Math. iii: 6.)

Dupin says: "They plunged those three times in the water when they baptized." (Hist. vol. 2, p. 77, 3d century.)

Paul Maria Paciandi, the great antiquarian, wrote a most learned book, which he dedicated to Pope Benedict XIV., and it was published by the authority of the Pope. He says of the representations of pouring on the head of the Savior, in the picture at Ravenna, that "Nothing can be more preposterous than these emblems. Was our Lord baptized by aspersion? This is so far from being true, that nothing can be more opposite to the truth, and it is to be attributed to the ignorance and rashness of workmen."

Dr. Joseph De Vicecomes, of Milan, says: "I will never cease to profess and teach that only immersion in water, except in cases of necessity, is lawful baptism in the church. I will refute that false notion that baptism was administered in the primitive church by pouring or sprinkling." (Ch. 6, Bk. 4.)

John Mabillon says that pouring "Was contrary to an express canon of the ninth century; contrary to the canon given by Stephen, which allowed pouring only in cases of necessity; contrary to the general practice in France, where trine immersion was used; contrary to the practice of the Spaniards, who used single immersion; contrary to the opinion of Alwin, who contended for trine immersion; and contrary to the practice of many who continued to dip until the fifteenth century." (Acta Sanc. Ord. Ben. par. ii. Proef: c. vii S. 186.)

Lewis Anthony Miratori, treating of the Ambrosian rite of baptism, as performed at Milan, says: "Observe the Ambrosian manner of baptizing. Now-a-days the priests preserve a shadow of the ancient Ambrosian form of baptizing, for they do not baptize by pouring, as the Romans do; but, taking the infant in their hands, they dip the hinder part of his head three times in the baptismal water, in the form of the cross, which is a vestige yet remaining of the most ancient and universal practice of immersion." (Atiq. Ital. Tom. iv. Dis. lxvii.)

Mattes says: "In regard to the ablution (in baptism) the present practice of the Latin Church differs altogether from that of the ancient church. We are accustomed to perform the ablution by sprinkling or by pouring water; but the apostles performed it by immersion, and this mode of baptism was the general practice until far into the Middle Ages." (Kirchen-Lexicon, art. Taufen of Wetzer and Welte.)

Catholic historians also declare that immersion was the general practice of the church for thirteen hundred years.

Dollinger says: "Baptism by immersion continued to be the prevailing practice of the church as late as the fourteenth century." (Hist. Ch. vol. 2, p. 295.)

Cardinal Gibbons, the foremost Catholic in the United States, says: "For several centuries after the establishment of Christianity, baptism was usually conferred by immersion; but since the twelfth century the practice of baptizing by affusion has prevailed in the Catholic Church, as this manner is attended with less inconvenience than baptism by immersion." (Faith of Our Fathers, p. 275.)

F. Brenner, in a very learned book, says: "Thirteen hundred years was baptism generally and ordinarily performed by the immersion of a man under water, and only in extraordinary cases was sprinkling or affusion permitted. These latter methods of baptism were called in question, and even prohibited." (Augusti, Denkwurd, vii, p. 68.)

There is a remarkable difference in the way Catholics and Protestants defend sprinkling. Protestants try to prove it from the Bible; but Catholics very frankly state that the Church changed the rite from immersion to sprinkling. Our Pedobaptist brethren have no answer to this statement of the case. The Catholic does not appeal to the Scripture, for it does not teach sprinkling; but the Church has authority over all ceremonies, and to him his position is impregnable. This could be proved by a multitude of authors, but two are sufficient.

Bishop Bossuet says: "The decision of Constance, in approbation of and for retaining communion under one kind, is one of those, wherein our adversaries think they have the most advantage. But in order to be convinced of the gravity and constancy of the Church in this decree, we need but remember that the Council of Constance, when they passed it, had found the custom of communicating under one kind established, beyond contradiction, many ages before. The case was much the same as that of baptism by immersion, as clearly grounded on Scripture as communion under both kinds could be, and which, nevertheless, *had been changed* into infusion, with as much ease and as little contradiction as communion under one kind was established, so that the same reason stood for retaining one as the other. It is a fact most certainly avowed in the Reformation, although some will cavil at it, that baptism was instituted by immersing the whole body into water; that Jesus Christ received it so, and caused it to be so given by his Apostles; that the Scripture knows no other baptism than this; that antiquity so understood and practiced it; that the word itself implies it, to baptize being the same as to dip; this fact, I say, is unanimously acknowledged by all the divines of the Reformation, nay, by the Reformers themselves, and those even who best understood the Greek language and the ancient customs as well of the Jews as Christians; by Luther, by Melancthon, by Calvin, by Casaubon, by Grotius, by all the rest, and lately even by Jurien, the most contradictory of all ministers. Nay, Luther has observed that the German word signifying baptism was derived from thence, and this sacrament named *Tauf*, from profundity or depth, because the baptized were deeply plunged into water." (Varia. Protest. vol. 2, p. 370.)

The same views prevail among Catholics in the United States. I wrote Cardinal Gibbons in regard to baptism, and he at once referred me to the work of Archbishop Kenrick on that subject as authoritative and as giving the information I desired. Archbishop Kenrick says: *"The change of discipline which has taken place to baptism* should not surprise us, for although the *Church* is but the dispenser of the sacraments which her Divine Spouse instituted, *she rightfully exercises a discretionary power* as to the manner of their administration. She can not change their substance. Baptism essentially consists of a washing with water under the invocation of the three Divine Persons. She can not substitute any other liquid, however precious, or any other formulary. The ablution can in no circumstances be dispensed with, but the manner of making it can be more or less solemn, according to her *wise discretion*. Immersion was well suited to the Eastern nations, whose habits and climate prepared them for it, and was therefore practiced in the commencement, whenever necessity did not prevent it. Cases, which at first were exceptional, gradually multiplied, so that at length the ordinary mode of baptism was by affusion. The *Church wisely sanctioned* that which, although less solemn, is equally effectual. *The power of binding and loosing,* which she received from Christ, *warrants this exercise of governing wisdom,* that the difference of times and places being considered, *condescension may be used* in regard to the mode of administering the sacraments without danger to their integrity. It is not for individuals to question a right which has been at all times claimed and exercised by those to whom the dispensation of the mysteries is divinely intrusted." (Kenrick on Bap. p. 174.)

In regard to the changing of the ordinance, one more quotation will be sufficient, because it was approved by their infallible Pope, Pius IX., and hence is maintained by all good Catholics. For whatever the Pope formally approves can be quoted as authoritative Catholic utterance. Pius IX. approved Haydock's notes on the Douay Bible. And the comment on Matt. iii: 6 is: "The

Church, which can not change the least article of faith, is not so tied up in matters of discipline and ceremony. Not only the Catholic Church, but also the pretended reformed churches, have altered the primitive custom in giving the sacrament of baptism, and now allow of baptism by sprinkling and pouring water upon the person baptized; nay, many of their ministers do it now-a-days by fillipping a wet finger and thumb over the child's head, which it is hard enough to call a baptizing in any sense."

While the Catholics now practice affusion because the Church changed the rite, they have no sympathy with that very foolish idea, "a drop is as good as an ocean," and with the flippant manner in which some persons administer the ordinance. In addition to the above from Haydock, I would commend this passage of Archbishop Kenrick to some of our friends: "Where no water is applied, it is absurd to suppose baptism; where the application of the water is scanty, and careless, as when a few drops are sprinkled toward a person, or the moist finger is slightly pressed on the forehead, there is great reason to fear that there is no baptism." (p. 5.)

CHAPTER XXVI.

WHAT THE EPISCOPALIANS SAY.

THE testimony of the Episcopalians is clear and conclusive as to the original manner of baptizing. There has been no hesitation among Episcopalian scholars in declaring that the Scriptures teach immersion. It was one of the last of the Pedobaptist churches that admitted sprinkling as baptism, and England was one of the very last countries that admitted sprinkling for baptism. Dr. Wall, a very learned Episcopalian, says:

"One would have thought that the cold countries should have been the first that should have *changed* the custom from dipping to affusion, because in cold climates the bathing of the body in water may seem much more unnatural and dangerous to the health than in hot ones (and it is to be noted, by the way, that all of those countries of whose rites of baptism, and immersion used in it, we have any account in the Scriptures or other ancient history, are in hot climates, where frequent and common bathing both of infants and grown persons is natural, and even necessary to the health). But by history it appears that the cold climates held the custom of dipping as long as any; for England, which is one of the coldest, was one of the latest that admitted this alteration of the ordinary way. . . . The offices or liturgies for public baptism in the Church of England did all along, so far as I can learn, enjoin dipping, without any mention of pouring or sprinkling. The *Manuele ad usum Sarum*, printed 1530, the 21st of Henry VIIIth, orders thus for the public baptisms: 'Then let the priest take the child and, having asked the name, baptize him by dipping him in the water thrice,' &c. And John Frith, writing in the year 1533 a Treatise of Baptism, calls the outward part of it the plunging down into it, and lifting up again; which he often mentions, without ever mentioning pouring or sprinkling. In the Common Prayer Book printed in 1549, the 2nd of King Edward VIth, the order stands thus: 'Shall dip it in the water thrice,' &c., 'so it be discreetly and warily done, saying, N, I baptize thee,' &c. But this order adds: 'And if the child be weak, it shall suffice to pour water upon it, saying the aforesaid words.' Afterward the book do leave out the word *thrice*, and do say, 'Shall dip it in the water, so it be discreetly,' &c., which *alteration*, I suppose, was made in the 6th of Edward the VIth, for then there was a new edition of the book, with some light alterations. And from thence it stood unaltered as to this matter to the 14th of Charles II." (Wall's Hist. Inft. Bap. vol 1, pp. 575, 579.)

There need be nothing more added to tell how sprinkling became the practice of the Episcopalian Church.

But as to the testimony of Episcopalians to the primitive act of baptism I could give innumerable names of the highest authority. I will have to content myself with a few selections. I shall begin with Dr. Wall, whom I have just quoted on another matter.

Dr. Wall says: "Their general and ordinary way was to baptize by immersion, or dipping the person, whether it was an infant or grown man or woman, into the water. This is so plain and clear from an infinite number of passages that, as one can not but pity the weak endeavors of such Pedobaptists as would maintain the negative of it, so also we ought to disown and show a dislike of the profane scoffs which some people give to the English anti-Pedobaptists merely for their use of dipping. It is one thing to maintain that that circumstance is not absolutely necessary to the essence of baptism, and another to go about to represent it as ridiculous and foolish, or as shameful and indecent; when it was, in all probability, the way by which our blessed Saviour, and for certain was the most usual and ordinary way by which the ancient Christians, did receive their baptism. I shall not stay to produce the particular proofs of this. Many of the quotations which I brought for other purposes, and do bring, do evince it. It is a great want of prudence, as well as of honesty, to refuse to grant to an adversary what is certainly true, and may be proved so. It creates a jealousy of all the rest, one says." (Hist. Inft. Bap. vol. 1, pp. 570, 571.)

B. H. Kennedy, late Professor of Greek, Cambridge, Eng., A. D. 1888, says: "That *baptizo* and its root word *bapto*, both of them, generally mean to dip, to immerse, is true; and upon this truth in part, in part upon the fact that our Lord and others, when baptized in the river Jordan, did go down into the water, and so were immersed, the Christian sect, commonly called Baptists, found their practices of immersion."

John Henry Blount, M. A., F. S. A., says: "It means dipping or bathing (Naaman, 2 Kings v: 14, and Judith xii: 7, LXX), the washing of cups and dishes (Mark vii: 3, Heb. ix: 10); also signifies overwhelming sorrows and sufferings (Isa. xxi: 4, LXX; Luke xii: 50, Matt. xx: 22). From all of which we may gather the meaning of a thorough cleansing, as by immersion or washing, and not by mere affusion or sprinkling of a few drops of water." (Dic. Doc. and His. Theol. Art. Bap.)

Charles Wheatly, in his recent work on the Book of Common Prayer, London, 1885, p. 349, says: "However, except upon extraordinary occasions, baptism was seldom, or perhaps never, administered for the first four centuries, but by immersion or dipping. Nor is aspersion or sprinkling ordinarily used, to this day, in any country that was never subject to the Pope. And among those that submitted to his authority, England was the last place where it was received. Though it has never obtained, so far as to be enjoined, *dipping* having been always prescribed by the rubric.'

Dean Stanley says: "Baptism was not only a bath, but a plunge—an entire submersion in the deep water, a leap as into the rolling sea or the rushing river, where for the moment the waves close over the bather's head, and he emerges again as from a momentary grave; or it was the shock of a shower bath—the rush of water passed over the whole person from capacious vessels, so as to wrap the recipient as within the vail of a splashing cataract. This was the part of the ceremony that the Apostles laid so much stress. It seemed to them like a burial of the old former self, and the rising up again of the new self. So St. Paul compared it to the Israelites passing through the roaring waves of the Red Sea, and St. Peter to the passing through the deep waters of the flood. 'We are buried,' said St. Paul, 'with Christ by baptism at his death; that like as Christ was raised, thus we also should walk in the newness of life.' Baptism, as the entrance into the Christian society, was a complete change from the old superstitions or restrictions of Judaism, to the freedom and confidence of the Gospel; from the idolatries and profligacies of the old heathen world to the light and purity of Christianity. It was a change effected only by the same effort and struggle as that with which a strong swimmer or an adventurous diver throws himself into the stream and struggles with the waves, and comes up with increased energy out of the depths of the dark abyss." (Christ. Inst. p. 7, 8.)

Bishop Ellicott says: "Jewish ablutions . . . had nothing in common with the figurative act which portrayed through immersion the complete disappearance of the old nature, and by emerging again, the beginning of a totally new life." (Life of Christ, p. 110.)

Dr. C. Geikie says: "It was, hence, impossible to see a convert go down into a stream, travel-

WHAT THE EPISCOPALIANS SAY. 219

worn, and soiled with dust, and, after disappearing for a moment, emerge pure and fresh, without feeling that the symbol suited and interpreted a strong craving of the human heart. It was no formal rite with John." (Life of Christ, p. 276.)

Dean Alford says: "The baptism was administered in the day time, by immersion of the whole person." (Gr. N. T., vol. 1, p. 20.)

Edersheim says: "It was as if symbolical, in the words of St. Peter (1 Pet. iii: 21), that baptism had been a flood, and he now emerged from it, ... indicative of a new life. Here, at these waters, was the kingdom into which Jesus had entered in the fulfillment of all righteousness; and from thence he emerged as its heaven designated, heaven qualified, and heaven proclaimed king." (Life of Christ, vol. 1, p. 284.)

There is a feeling on the part of a great many eminent Episcopalians to restore the primitive immersion among them. This is advocated by many of their foremost men. In 1861, Mr. Crystal published a book on "The modes of Christian Baptism," in which he ardently defended the return of the Episcopal Church to immersion as the act of baptism. Among other things he said: "It is evident, 1. That if we restore immersion, we only restore what has ever been our theory, so far back as the history of the Anglican Church extends. We correct only a late and not primitive practice. 2. Should we restore the trine immersion as the general practice, we should have good reason to lay claim to the only mode which, so far as we can judge from all the testimony which the early church affords, can lay historically attested claim to being the normal mode of the Apostles." (p. 213.)

Bishop Smith, of Kentucky, was a defender of immersion. Said he: "We have only to go back six or eight hundred years, and immersion was the only mode, except in case of the few baptized on their beds when death was near. And with regard to such cases, it disqualified its recipient for holy orders in case he recovered. Immersion was not only universal six or eight hundred years ago, but it was *primitive* and *apostolic*, no case of baptism standing on record by any other mode for the first three hundred years, except the few cases of those baptized clinically, lying in bed. If any one practice of the early church is clearly established, it is immersion." But Bishop Smith was not satisfied with a mere statement of the case; he desired a restoration of the primitive practice. Accordingly, he immersed his own infant child, having previously declared it advisable to send some

Episcopalians to Greece, that they might obtain immersion from those who had practiced it in regular succession from the Apostles, and on their return restore the practice quietly and without noise throughout his communion. (Kenrick on Bap. p. 150.)

I have before me a noble letter from the most scholarly Bishop of the Episcopal Church in America—Bishop A. Cleveland Coxe, Buffalo, New York. He is the editor of that learned work that has just come from the press—The Ante-Nicene Fathers. While I differ from him in some statements, he does say that "dip" is the meaning of the word baptize; and, further, that the primitive rite of dipping should be restored in all Christian churches. This is in every way so remarkable that I give his letter entire:

Buffalo, N. Y., April 16th, 1890.

Rev. and Dear Sir,—Yours of the 31st ult. came to hand at the very busiest season of our "Christian year." I have had no time since then to answer half of my letters. I laid yours aside, hoping to find a spare hour to reply to it, as it merits. I dare not wait any longer, and must therefore answer in few words, as follows:

1. The word means to dip.
2. I think the "sacred writers" used the word

in the primary sense, but also for other washings which were not dippings. So did also the classical writers, with great freedom and variety of meanings.

3. In the Church of England dipping is even now the primary rule. But it is not the ordinary custom. It survived far down into Queen Elizabeth's time, but seems to have died out early in the seventeenth century. It never has become obsolete. I, myself, have baptized by dipping both adults and babes.

I ought to add that in France (unreformed) the custom of dipping became obsolete long before it was disused in England. But for this *bad example* my own opinion is that dipping would still prevail among Anglicans.

I wish that all Christians would restore the primiive practice. I say this, tho' I believe the other to be valid—as in the case of clinic baptism—in in early Christian history.

In Christ your friend and Brother,

A. CLEVELAND COXE.

CHAPTER XXVII.

WHAT THE PRESBYTERIANS SAY.

AS to the original act of baptism, the scholarship of the Presbyterian Church has all been on one side. They declare that the original act of baptism was immersion. I shall present the statements of some Presbyterians and give some history in this chapter.

John Calvin, the father of the Presbyterian Church, never failed to testify that baptism was an immersion in water. Says he: "The word baptize signifies to immerse, and it is certain that the rite of immersion was observed by the ancient church." (Inst. Book 4, c. 15.)

Beza, who was a colleague of Calvin, testifies: "Christ commanded us to be baptized, by which word it is certain immersion is signified." "To be baptized in water signifies no other than to be immersed in water, which is the external ceremony of baptism."

Zwingle, another of Calvin's associates, said: "When ye were immersed into the water of baptism, ye were engrafted into the death of Christ; that is, the immersion of your body into water was a sign that ye ought to be engrafted into Christ and his death, that as Christ died and was buried, ye also may be dead to the flesh and the old man, that is, to yourselves." (Com. Rom. vi: 3.)

Dr. John Diodati, of Geneva, one of the most learned men of his times and a member of the Synod of Dort, says of the baptism of John: "Plunged in the water for a sacred sign and seal of the expiation and remission of sins." (Annotat. 1648, p. 6, vol. 2.) On Rom. vi: 3, he says: "In baptism, being dipped in water according to the ancient ceremony, it is a sacred figure to us that sin ought to be drowned in us by God's Spirit." (Vol 2, p. 158.)

Although these early Presbyterians were thus positive about the apostolic act of baptism, they erred in not following what they confessed the Scriptures thus plainly taught. Calvin took the ground that it was a matter of no consequence, and that churches ought to be left at liberty on this question. No flood gate was ever opened wider, and innumerable have been the evils that have followed from this position. I will give his theory in his own words, as they are sufficiently explicit: "Wherefore the Church did grant liberty to herself, since the beginning, *to change the rites* somewhat, excepting the substance. *It is of no consequence* at all whether the person that is baptized is totally immersed, or whether he is merely sprinkled by an affusion of water. This should be *a matter of choice* to the churches in different regions." This is exactly the Roman Catholic position, and will always end in direct disobedience to the commands of Jesus Christ.

In another chapter I have shown some of the practical workings of this thing. John Knox and many others were compelled to flee from Scotland during the reign of bloody Mary, and they sought an asylum at Geneva. Here they enthusiastically accepted the views of John Calvin. When they returned home they carried these opinions with them. They at once advocated affusion for baptism instead of immersion. This idea slowly grew, and the people were much divided. At length, when the Westminster Assembly of Divines met to frame a creed and government for the Presbyterian Church, sprinkling was carried over immersion by one vote. The vote stood 25 to 24. The Presbyterian Church came this near forever practicing the apostolic act of baptism, and yet there be some who defend sprinkling on the ground of its being scriptural. It was only through the influence of Dr. Lightfoot, who was President of the Assembly, that sprinkling was admitted at all.

These are such interesting statements that I will give the transaction in the words of Dr. Lightfoot himself. He was the principal actor in the matter and kept a journal, and so his testimony may be reckoned unbiased. Dr. Lightfoot said: "Then we fell upon the work of the day, which was about baptizing 'of the child, whether to dip him or to sprinkle.' And this proposition, 'It is lawful and sufficient to besprinkle the child,' had been canvassed before our adjourning, and was ready now to vote; but I spake against it, as being very unfit to vote; that it is lawful to sprinkle when every one grants it. Whereupon it was fallen upon, sprinkling being granted, whether dipping should be tolerated with it. And here fell we upon a large and long discourse, whether dipping were essential, or used in the first institution, or in the Jews' custom. Mr. Coleman went about, in a large discourse, to prove *tbilh* to be dipping overhead. Which I answered at large. After a long dispute, it was at last put to the question, whether the Directory should run thus, 'The minister shall take water, and sprinkle or pour it with his hand upon the face or forehead of the child;' and it was voted so indifferently, that we were glad to count names twice; for so many were so unwilling to have dipping excluded, that the votes came to an equality within one; for the one side were 24, the other 25, the 24 for the reserving of dipping, and the 25 against it; and there grew a great heat upon it, and when we had done all, we concluded upon nothing in it, but the business was recommitted."

"Aug. 8th. But as to the dispute itself about dipping, it was thought safe and most fit to let it alone, and to express it thus in our Directory: 'He is to baptize the child with water, which for the manner of doing is not only lawful, but also sufficient, and most expedient to be by pouring or sprinkling of water on the face of the child, without any other ceremony.' But this lost a great deal of time about the wording of it." (Works, vol. 13, p. 299, London 1824.)

Thus was affusion established in the Prebyterian Church. To say the least, this is a very remarkable history.

But notwithstanding this the foremost scholars have always conceded that immersion is baptism. I shall present the names of only a few, but they are all representative men.

I begin with the great Turretin, who was a Professor of Theology in Geneva. He says: "For as in baptism when performed in the primitive manner, by immersion and emersion, descending into the water, and again going out of it, of which descent and ascent we have an example in the eunuch, Acts viii: 38, 39; yea, and what is more, as by this rite, when persons are immersed in water, they are overwhelmed and, as it were, buried, and in a manner buried together with Christ, and again they emerge, seem to be raised out of the grave, and are said to be risen again with Christ." (Works, vol. 3, p. 326, Edinburg ed. 1847.)

Richard Baxter, and the Presbyterians never had a greater man, says: "It is commonly confessed by us to the Anabaptists, as our commentators declare, that in the Apostles' time the baptized were dipped over head in the water, and this signified their profession, both of believing the burial and the resurrection of Christ, and of their own renouncing the world and flesh, or dying to sin and living to Christ, or rising again to newness of life, or being buried and risen again with Christ, as the Apostle expounded in the forecited texts of Col. and Rom. And though (as before said) we have thought it lawful to disuse the manner of dipping, and to use less water, yet we presume not to change the use and signification of it." (Dis. Right to Sac. p. 70.)

Dr. Chalmers, after saying, "the original meaning of the word baptism is immersion," remarks: "Let it never be forgotten of the Particular Baptists of England that they form the denomination of Fuller and Carey and Ryland and Hall and Foster; that they have originated among the greatest of all missionary enterprises; that they have enriched the Christian literature of our country with authorship of the most exalted piety, as well as the first talent and the first eloquence; that they have waged a very noble and successful war with the hydra of Antinomianism; that perhaps there is not a more intellectual community of ministers in our island, or who have put forth to their number a greater amount of mental power and mental activity in the defense and illustration of our common faith; and, what is better than all of the triumphs of genius or understanding, who, by their zeal and fidelity and pastoral labor among the congregations which they have reared, have done more to swell the lists of genuine discipleship in the walks of private society, and thus to uphold and to extend the living Christianity of our nation." (On Rom. Lec. 14, p. 76.)

Dr. Lyman Coleman, for many years Professor in Lafayette College, Pa., says: "We can not resist the conviction that this mode of baptism was the first departure from the teaching and example of the Apostles on this subject. . . . . It was a departure from their teachings; it was the earliest, for immersion was unquestionably very early the common mode of baptism." (Ancient Chris. Ex. p. 366.)

Dr. George Campbell was one of the most scholarly men the Presbyterians ever had. He says: "I have heard of a disputant of this stamp, in defiance of *etymology* and *use*, maintain that the word rendered in the New Testament baptize means more properly to sprinkle than to plunge; and, in defiance of all antiquity, that the former method was the earliest, and for many centuries the most general practice in baptizing. One who argues in this manner never fails, with persons of knowledge, to betray the cause he would defend; and though, in respect to the vulgar, bold assertions generally succeed as well as arguments, sometimes better, yet a candid mind will disdain to take the help of a falsehood even in support of the truth." (Lect. on Pul. El. Lect. 10, pp. 294, 295.)

Philip Schaff, D. D., LL. D., Professor of Church History in the Union Theological Seminary, New York, says: "The baptism of Christ in the river of Jordan, and the illustrations of baptism used in the New Testament, are all in favor of immersion rather than sprinkling, as is freely admitted by the best exegetes, Catholic and Protestant, English and German. *Nothing can be gained by unnatural exegesis. The aggressiveness of the Baptists has driven Pedobaptists to the opposite extreme.*" (Teach. pp. 55, 56.)

I have at hand a fresh and new statement of the case. The Southern Presbyterians of the United States have founded three churches in Greece, and all three of them practice immersion. Dr. W. D. Powell, of Mexico, recently wrote from Athens, Greece, as follows: "I found that all churches in Greece—the Presbyterians included—are compelled to immerse candidates for baptism, for, as one of the professors remarked, 'the commonest day laborer understands nothing else for *baptizo* but immersion.' Some Greeks who have made fortunes in other countries have built and equipped some fine schools and colleges, as well as museums, &c. The university has 3000 students, of whom 1200 are preparing to be doctors and lawyers. I visited the university and saw the magnificent library and museum. I asked a professor what *baptizo* meant, and he said: 'It has but one meaning—to submerge, to immerse. Why do you ask?'"

In reply to an editorial in the *Christian Observer*, of Louisville, Ky., Dr. Powell writes to the *West-*

ern Recorder, Jan 8th, 1891, as follows: "I asked Bro. Sakellarios, who has charge of the Baptist Church in Athens, if the Greek word could mean any thing but immersion, and he said 'No.' To my inquiry how the Presbyterians managed this question, he replied: 'Very easily—by having a baptistery made, in which they immerse infants just as the Greek priests do.' Said he: 'Once they sprinkled some children, and it created such a scandal that it came near breaking up the church, and they were compelled to have a small baptistery made.' Adult Greeks are received into the Presbyterian Church on the baptism which they received in the Greek Church. In Greece, Bulgaria, Asia Minor, Syria, Palestine, and wherever the Greek language is spoken, immersion for baptism is practiced."

Here is an instance where the Presbyterians practice what their scholars preach. This is the land where Greek is a living language, and nothing but immersion is practiced there. This little statement does away with many a ponderous article written by our Presbyterian brethren to explain and defend their practice on this subject. We commend this to our Presbyterian brethren.

CHAPTER XXVIII.

WHAT THE METHODISTS SAY.

I HAVE been examining Mr. Wesley's works, and will give the result of my investigation. Turning to his journal, vol. 1, p. 20, under date of Saturday, February 21st, 1736, Mr. Wesley says: "Mary Welch, aged eleven days, was *baptized according to the custom of the first church,* and *the rule of the Church of England, by immersion.* The child was ill then, but *recovered* from that very hour."

Three things are evident from this: 1. The early church practiced immersion. 2. That this was the practice of the Church of England; and 3. That this is positively opposed to the doctrine of some circuit riders who say that immersion destroys health. Before this objection is offered again they must change the "standards," as they have often done before, and make Mr. Wesley cease to say, "the child was ill then, but recovered from that very hour."

The next instance occurred in Savannah, Ga., May 5th, 1736, and is most significant. Mr. Wesley says: "I was asked to baptize a child of Mr.

Parker's, second bailiff of Savannah; but Mrs. Parker told me, neither Mr. P. nor I will consent to its being dipped! I answered, if you certify that your child is weak, it will suffice (the rubric says) to pour water upon it. She replied: 'Nay, the child is not weak, but I am resolved that it shall not be dipped.' This argument I could not refute, so I went home and the child was baptized by another person. (Journal, vol. 1, p. 24.) But this was not the end of the matter. On the first day of September, 1737, Mr. Wesley was tried by a grand jury of forty-four men, found guilty, and ordered to leave the country. I will let Mr. Wesley state the charges. He says: "Therein they asserted, upon oath, that John Wesley, clerk, had broken the laws of the realm, contrary to the peace of our sovereign lord the King, his honor and dignity.

1. By speaking and writing to Mrs. Williamson, against her husband's consent.

2. By repelling her from the holy communion.

3. By not declaring his adherence to the Church of England.

4. By dividing the morning services of Sundays.

5. By refusing to baptize Mr. Parker's child, otherwise than by dipping, except the parents

would certify that it was weak, and not able to bear it.

6. For repelling William Gough from the holy communion.

7. By refusing to read the burial services over the body of Nathaniel Polhill.

8. By calling himself ordinary of Savannah.

9. By refusing to receive William Aglionby, as god-father, only because he was not a communicant.

10. For refusing Jacob Matthews for the same reason; and baptizing an Indian trader's child with only two sponsors. (This, I own, was wrong; for I ought, at all hazards, to have refused baptizing it till he had procured a third.)" (Journal, vol. 1, pp. 42, 43.)

This is a strange record for the father of the Methodists. John Wesley was tried and found guilty by the courts of the land for refusing to sprinkle a baby! Dr. Watson, in his Life of Wesley, professes to give a fair account of this trial of Wesley, and yet he says not a word about this child He mentions a few of the most trivial charges, and altogether treats the trial as a small affair. Does not this look like trying to conceal an important fact? And talk of close communion.

No Baptist of my acquaintance has ever "repelled" a man and a woman from the Lord's table.

On June the 25th, he re-baptized John Smith; and March 21st, 1759, he baptized two adults by immersion." (Journal, vol. 2, p. 16.)

I have heard men speak very largely upon the figurative use of the word baptize; baptized in wine, sleep, dews of heaven, etc. But all such persons need to do is to turn to Mr. Wesley's Journal, vol. 2, p. 152, and read of a certain man "who was wet all over with sweat as if he had been dipped in water."

In the old Discipline, compiled by Wesley, Jesus was baptized in the river of Jordan, and the sixth of Romans means simply a burial in water. On the baptism of suffering, Mark x: 38, he says: "Our Lord was filled with sufferings, and covered with them without."

I now turn to Wesley's Notes on the New Testament, and under Rom. vi: 3, I read: "We are buried with him, alluding to the ancient manner of baptizing by immersion."

Adam Clarke follows Wesley in his admissions. He says, in reference to the baptism of John: "That the baptism of John was by plunging the body (after the same manner as the washing unclean persons, and the baptism of proselytes was), seems

WHAT THE METHODISTS SAY.

to appear from those things that are related of him; namely, that he baptized in Jordan, that he baptized in Enon, because there was much water there; and that Christ being baptized came up out of the water; to which that seems to be parallel, Acts, viii: 38, Philip and the eunuch went down into the water," &c. (Com. vol. 3, p. 344.)

In his comment on Rom. vi: 4, he says: "We are buried with him by baptism into death. It is probable that the apostle alludes to the mode of administering baptism by immersion, the whole body being put under water, which seems to say the man is drowned, is dead; and, when he came up out of the water, he seemed to have a resurrection to life; the man is risen again, he is alive. He was, therefore, supposed to throw off his old gentile state, as he threw off his clothes, and to assume a new character, as the baptized generally put on a new or fresh garment." (Com. vol. 4, p. 78.)

On Colossians ii: 12, Clarke says: "Alluding to the immersion practiced in the case of adults, wherein the person appeared to be buried under the water, as Christ was buried in the heart of the earth. His rising again the third day, and their emerging from the water, was an emblem of the resurrection of the body, and, in them, of a total change of life." (Com. vol. 4, p. 538.)

Gregory and Ruter say in their Church History: "The initiatory rite of baptism was usually performed by immersing the whole body in the baptismal font, and in the earlier years of Christianity was permitted to all who acknowledged the truths of the Gospel and promised conformity to its laws." (Hist. p. 34.) Of the second century they say: "Baptism was publicly performed twice a year. The catechumens (or probationers for baptism) assembled in the church on the great festivals of Easter and Whitsuntide; and after a public declaration of their faith, and a solemn assurance from their sponsors that it was their intention to live conformably to the Gospel, they received the sacrament of baptism. This rite was performed by three immersions and the body was divested of clothes. In order to preserve decency in the operation, the baptismal font of the women was separated from that of the men, and they were as much as possible attended by the deaconnesses of the church." (Church Hist. p. 53.)

I have before me a very recent book, 1889, from the Methodist press. It is called Christian Archæology, by Charles W. Bennett, D.D. It is edited by George R. Crooks, D.D., and Bishop John F.

Hurst. The preface announces that "the theology of the" volume is in "harmony with the standards of the Methodist Episcopal Church." This is certainly authoritative as well as fresh. Dr. Bennett says: "The customary mode was used by the apostles in the baptism of the first converts. They were familiar with the baptism of John's disciples and of the Jewish proselytes. This was ordinarily by dipping or immersion. This is indicated not only by the general signification of the words used in describing the rite, but the earliest testimony of the documents which have been preserved gives preference to this mode. . . . . The terms of Scripture describing the rite, most of the figures used by the writers of the New Testament to indicate its significance (Rom. vi: 4; Col. ii: 12, et al.), the explanations of the Apostolic Constitutions, the comments of the foremost Christian fathers for the first six centuries, and the express instructions of ecclesiastical councils, indicate that immersion was the more usual mode of baptism." (Chris. Arch. pp. 396, 397.)

The scholarship of the Methodist Church joins with that of all others in proclaiming that immersion is apostolic.

CHAPTER XXIX.

WHAT THE SYRIAC SAYS.

ONE of the oldest, if not the oldest, translation of the New Testament is that of the Peshito Syriac. It was made in the second century in the very country where the apostles lived and wrote. It is regarded by scholars as one of the best translations of the New Testament ever made. From these considerations the Syriac is of much importance.

The word used in the Syriac to translate the Greek word baptize is *amad*. It has been claimed by some that *amad* means "to stand." Gesenius defines the Hebrew word which corresponds with *amad* "to stand," and adds: "In the Syriac Church *amad* is 'to baptize,' perhaps because the person to be baptized stood in the water; but see Castell Lex. ed. Michaelis sub verbo." This standing up in the water suits the idea of immersion rather than that of sprinkling or pouring; for certainly no one "stands in the water" to receive sprinkling or pouring. If the word means to stand, sprinkle or pour can not be a direct translation of it.

WHAT THE SYRIAC SAYS. 241

If I was forced to the conclusion that the Syriac *amad* must be limited to the idea of standing, I should prefer to regard it as meaning "to take a stand," and so to make the public profession. Baptism is the appointed method of professing to be a Christian, and the word indicating the thing accomplished by baptism may have come to be used for the act of baptism itself. This position is suggested by eminent Pedobaptist scholars. Dr. Isaac H. Hall, of the Metropolitan Museum of Art, New York, one of the foremost Syriac scholars of our country, writes me under date of February 7, 1891: "I think the word was originally the same as the Hebrew and the Arabic, and that it meant *to stand, to set up*. Baptizing was thus taking a stand or position as one of the visible church. Thence used to render *baptizein*, it obtained finally the meaning *to dip, or to immerse*." If this is the meaning of the word, I have only to observe two things: 1. In that view it primarily gives no indication as to the act of baptism, but by usage the word came to mean to dip; and 2. That it explicitly disagrees with the baptism of infants who do not "take a stand," or make any personal profession, any more than they "stand up in the water" to be baptized. So the word in that understanding of it gives no aid to our Pedobaptist brethren. It does not help them as to the act, and it is distinctly opposed to their teaching as to the subjects.

The view, however, which seems to be the most probable is, that the Syriac word means to immerse. It is claimed by B. Davies, in his Hebrew Lexicon, that besides the ordinary Hebrew word *amad*, meaning "to stand," there is a second root, spelled and pronounced exactly like it, and meaning "to sink," and so to be overwhelmed. Fürst, in his lexicon, gives *amad* three times, as three separate roots; the first being the ordinary one "to stand," the second "to waver," and the third "to be inclined, to lean to a thing, to turn to one side," and from this third root he derives the common Hebrew preposition *immad*.

Without going into any discussion as to the root of the word *amad* in Hebrew in these various senses, which is only indirectly in line with our investigations, it is sufficient to say that all Syriac lexicons recognize immerse as the natural meaning of the Syriac word *amad*.

I present the testimony of the lexicons:

Castell says: "To bathe, to baptize, to immerse." (Lex. Heptaglot sub. vc. London, 1669.)

Buxtorf says: "To baptize, to dip, to bathe, to bathe oneself." (Lex. Chal. and Syr. Basle, 1622.)

Guido Fabricus says: "To baptize, to dip, to wash." (Ant. Poly. sub. vc. Antwerp, 1592.)

Michaelis says: "To bathe, to baptize, to immerse." He adds: "In this signification of baptizing not a few compare with the Hebrew *amadstetit* (he stood), so that *stare* is *stare in flumine, illoque mergi* (to stand in the river, and in it to be immersed). To me it seems more probable that it is altogether different from the Hebrew *amad*, and has arisen through some permutation of the letters from the (Arabic) *amath, submergere* (to submerge). The signification of standing, common to the other Oriental tongues, I do not find among the Syrians, save in the derivative *amud*, and which is cited from Castell from one place (Ex. xiii: 22), but which you will find is read almost everywhere in Hebrew pillar of cloud and pillar of fire."

Gutbier, in the small lexicon affixed to his edition of the Syriac New Testament, gives the meaning, "to baptize, he was baptized, he upheld." This last meaning has no reference to support it, and it is apparently introduced only with the purpose of deriving from this sense of the verb the noun *amud*, which means a column. With this exception I do not find in any Syriac lexicon the expression to stand, or any similar expression, given as a signification of the Syriac word *amad*.

Bernstein says: "To immerse, to be immersed, to immerse oneself." (Chres. Syr. Leipzig, 1836, p. 378.)

The latest and most authoritative of all the Syriac lexicons is that of R. Payne Smith, published last year in England. G. B. Bernstein, of Germany, gathered much material for such a work during his laborious life, and at his death this material passed into the hands of Dean Smith. Now, after years of work, and with the co-operation of the foremost Syriac scholars of the world, Dean Smith has published his "Thesaurus Syriacus." He defines *amad*: "to descend, to be immersed, to be baptized."

The testimony of these seven lexicons is conclusive. There is not the most distant intimation that these scholars ever thought that *amad* meant to sprinkle or to pour.

The use of the word by Syriac scholars is in accord with this idea. All through the Syriac Bible *amad* is used to translate the Greek *baptizo*; and *amad* is used ten times in the sense of to dip in the Syriac Bible where the ordinance of baptism is not referred to, and where, therefore, it must be used in the ordinary and non-ecclesiastical sense. This fact is sufficient to clothe with shame those who adduce this Syrian word as an argument against immersion. The word is frequently used in Syriac literature in the sense of to dip, as a diver after pearls, of the setting sun, the entering of an arrow into the brain, the three Hebrew children into the fire, he dipped his mouth into the water, &c.

Ephraem Syrus, of Edessa, speaks of the baptism of Christ in a way that must include an immersion. "How wonderful," says he, "that thy footsteps were planted on the waters, that the great sea should submit itself to thy feet, and that yet at a small river that same head of thine should be subjected to be bowed down and baptized in it."

I add an array of authority that is impregnable.

Theodore Beza says that *baptizo* means to immerse, and adds: "Nor does the signification of *amad*, which the Syrians use for baptize, differ at all from this." (Annot. in Mark vii: 4.)

Casparis Clavor, after quoting the Syriac for Rom. vi: 4, adds: "Which may be translated 'in baptism,' beyond all doubt referring not to baptismal sprinkling, but to immersion." (Anniversarium Dodec., Leipzig, 1719.)

Dr. John Mason Neale, the greatest Anglican connoisseur of the Greek Church, says: "All the

Syrian forms prescribe or assume trine immersion." (Hist. East. Ch., p. 949.)

Some years ago Dr. C. H. Toy, Professor of Oriental Literature in Harvard University, wrote a work upon "*Amad.*" His conclusions were: "From our inquiry it appears that there were no cases in which *amad* may not mean *dip*, and some in which it must have that meaning: that there are similar verbs in Arabic meaning the same thing: that the verb *amad*, 'to stand,' probably disappeared from the Syriac language some centuries before Christ: that it is not satisfactorily explained how a meaning *baptize* could come from a meaning *stand:* and that all authorities in Syriac concur in assigning to *amad* the signification *dip*."

I recently wrote Dr. Toy and asked him if more recent research had confirmed him in these conclusions. He replied:

CAMBRIDGE, Mass., January 29, 1891.

DR. J. T. CHRISTIAN:

Dear Sir,—Your enquiry of the 24th has been received. My conclusion was that the stem *amad* in Syriac, signifies "to be dipped." In addition to the authorities there quoted, I can now cite the great "Thesaurus Syriacus," edited by Payne Smith, with the co-operation of many scholars; in this most recent publication (which appeared last year) *amad* is defined as—"*descendit, mersus est, baptizatus est.*" Yours truly,

C. H. TOY.

It is with genuine pleasure that I am able to present the additional testimony of Dr. Gottheil, of Columbia College, New York; Dr. R. Payne Smith, the Dean of Canterbury, England, and the author of the great Syriac Lexicon; and of Prof. Th. Nöldeke, Strasburg, Germany, who is a recognized authority in Syriac the world over. The testimony of these men is most decisive.

Dr. Gottheil says:

COLUMBIA COLLEGE, N. Y., March 21, 1890.

My Dear Sir:—

1. The Syriac word you refer to, *amad*, means really to go down, decline, immerse one's self, (*e. g.* the day declines).

2. It is used in the sense of *baptizein* continually in the New Testament.

3. It is from the Arabic glamada, "to put a thing within something else," (*e. g.*, a sword in its sheath). Believe me, very truly yours,

RICHARD GOTTHEIL.

Dean Smith writes:

DEANERY, CANTERBURY, March 20, 1891.

THE REV. J. T. CHRISTIAN, D.D.

Dear Sir,—The strict meaning of *amad* is to go down, descend. It is used of the sun setting, etc., and secondly to going down into a brook, river, etc., to wash. The word for baptism is the Aphel or Causative form, literally *to cause to descend, immerse, dip*, either totally or partially. In this sense the verb is used in the Syriac New Testament and in all ecclesiastical writers for baptize. It answers to the Greek *baptizein* in the sense of washing one's self. The Aphel is seldom used in any other sense than that of baptism; but it is used of dipping a bell into water, but possibly as a sort of religious ceremony.

Believe me, very truly yours,

R. PAYNE SMITH.

Prof. Th. Nöldeke writes:

STRASBURG, GERMANY, February 17th, 1891.

DR. J. T. CHRISTIAN, *Jackson, Miss.:*

Dear Sir,—*Amad* signifies, as is declared with entire correctness by Payne Smith, primarily *to draw down, to go under, to immerse one's self.* In the New Testament it is used with entire regularity for *baptizesthai,* and always in the passive sense: therefore, it is connected with the Syriac *men-von-hupo*. (Math. iii: 13.) By all Syrians it is the regular word for being baptized. The Christian inhabitants of Palestine, who spoke another dialect, have a different word, *Atbal;* which word is also found in use among the Mandeans, a peculiar sect in Babylonia, which took its origin in part only from Christianity. This word, however, signifies immerse (eintauchen).

I am inclined to believe that John and Jesus, as residents of Palestine, used the word *atbal* or *tabal* for baptize, and that the word *amad*, which extended from Edessa all over Syria, was employed to set forth Christian opposition against the usage of the Jewish Christian party. That, however, is nothing more than a supposition. I would remark, in addition, that baptize in the active voice is expressed by the causative *amad*. The Jewish word for the baptismal bath is *Hetbil*.

Very respectfully,
TH. NÖLDEKE.

I, therefore, justly arrive at the conclusion that *amad* means to dip.

THE END.

INDEX OF AUTHORS AND SUBJECTS.

	PAGE
Achilles, Tatius	28
Admissions of Pedobaptist Scholars	13–15
Ænon, Baptism of	50
Age, The	195
Alabaster	142
Alcibiades	24
Alciphron	26
Alcuin	76, 117
Alexander, Dr. Gross	16
Alford, Dean	219
Ambrose, Bishop	116
Apostolic Constitutions	121
Aquinas, Thomas	134, 159, 204
Aratus	186
Argonautic Expedition	28
Ariosto	184
Aristophen	27
Arnoldi	205
Augustine, Bishop	117, 150
Augustine	77, 79
Avitus, Bishop	76
Badger	177
Barnabas	108, 125
Barnes, Albert	87, 106
Baronius	148, 155
Basnage	153
Basil	113
Bass	19
Baxter, Richard	228

	PAGE
Beaulieu, Madleine de	176
Beds, Baptism of	68
Benardus de Montfaucon	37
Bennett, Dr. C. W.	48, 52, 72, 106, 147, 202, 238
Bernardino	144
Beza	223, 245
Bickersteth	187, 188, 190
Bjerring, Rev. Nicholas	198
Blackstone	8
Blount, John Henry	216
Bonaventura	204
Boniface, St.	79
Bonwetsch, Prof	198
Bossuet, Bishop	208
Brazen Vessels	67
Brenner, F	208
Brewster, Sir David	158, 160, 163
Britannica Encyclopædia	41
Brown	9, 10, 12, 13
Bryennios, Bishop	119, 122
Bullinger, E. W	19
Bunsen, Baron	111
Buried with Christ	102
Burnstein	244
Buxtorf	36, 242
Calcuith, Council of	169, 170
Calvin, John	51, 84, 162, 163, 210, 223, 224, 225, 238

(251)

INDEX.

	PAGE		PAGE
Camden	78	Cyclades, Bishop of	197
Campbell, Dr. George. 52, 65, 66, 115,	230	Cyprian 116, 131, 152,	156
		Cyril of Jerusalem	54
Carthage, Council of	168		
Cashel, Council of	172	Dale, J. W	32
Casaubon	35	Dante 182,	183
Castello, E 36, 240,	242	Davies 36,	242
Catholics, Testimony of	204	Delitzsch, Franz	45
Cave	73	Demetrius	26
Cereas	195	Demoleon, M	179
Cerfee, Lexicon of	196	Demosthenes	24
Chalmers, Dr 104,	229	Didache	119
Chariton	28	Dill, J. S	101
Christian Baptism	57	Diodati	224
Chrysostom 73, 74,	113	Diodorus	25
Clarke, Adam ... 48, 106,	236	Dion Cassius	26
Classical Baptism	23	Dionysius	113
Clavor	245	Discipline, Methodist.181,	251
Clermont, Council of	173	Dobbs, C. E. W	129
Clinic Baptism	151	Doddridge, Dr 51,	84
Clough, J. E	82	Döllinger, Dr. 49, 72, 134, 204,	207
Clovis, King	75		
Coke 12,	13	Donnegan	20
Cold Countries	161	Drown, does *baptizo* mean to	31
Coleman, Lyman	229		
Collier	170	Dryden	186
Cologne, Council of	174	Dupin	205
Conant, T. J	32	Durant, Guillaume	179
Conon	25		
Conybeare and Howson 37, 91, 96,	107	Eaton, T. T	98
		Ellicott, Bishop....54, 66, 85, 97,	218
Cooly	10		
Councils	167	Endersheim	219
Cowper 30, 93,	185	Epictetus	26
Cox, Homersham 85,	131	Episcopalians, testimony of	213
Coxe, Bishop A. Cleveland 21, 122,	221		
		Est, Chancellor	105
Cremer	19	Eubulus	24
Crystal	219	Eulogius	77

INDEX. 253

	PAGE		PAGE
Eunuch, The	83, 115	Gregory of Tours	76
Eusebius	151, 152, 154, 155	Groves	20
Eustathius	29	Gutbier	243
Evenus	24		
		Hak-Kodesh, Rabbi	40
Fabyan	77	Hall, Dr. Isaac H	241
Fabrycus	243	Harnack, Adolf	33, 123, 124, 129
Farrar	107, 119	Hart	170, 172, 174
Fathers, Greek	23, 108	Haydock	211
Fathers, Latin	114	Heaton	47
Felsenthal, Rabbi B	42	Hebrew lexicons, testimony of	36
Figurative Meanings	30, 38	Hedericus	19
Fisher, George P	107, 131	Heimerius	27
Fleet, Dr. A. F	192	Heliodorus	28
Fradensdorf, J. W	18	Henry	77
Frith, John	179	Hersman, C. C	17
Fritzche	35	Hibbard, Dr	41, 59, 96
Funk, Dr	135	Hilgenfeld, Prof	133
Geikie, C	49, 218	Hincmar	77
Giesler	154	Hippocrates	32, 34
Gesenius	36–39, 86, 240	Hippolytus	111
Gibbons, Cardinal	207, 210	History, testimony of	128
Gibbs	36	Hodge, C	8
Gilbert, Bishop	75	Hodge, C. W	17
Glogan, Ritual	178	Hogue, Prof. Addison	193
Gocelyn	78	Holtzman, Prof	66, 133
Gothic Missal	176	Holy Spirit, baptism of	51
Gottheil, R	247	Homer	90, 92, 186
Gould, S. Baring	143	Homeric Allegories	23
Gratus, Bishop	168	Humphreys, Prof. M. W.	31
Greek Church	192	Hurst, Bishop	48, 106, 202
Ancient and Modern Greek	192–195	Irenæus	110
Greek Ritual	181, 195		
Green	20		
Greenfield	16, 20	Jahn	68
Greenleaf	7, 8, 11, 13	Jailer's baptism	94
Gregory Pope	77, 169, 180	Jerome	117, 118
Gregory, Thaumaturgus	112	Jesus, baptism of	56

INDEX.

John the Baptist........ 46
Jonathan................ 38
Josephus............25, 34
Julian.,..............28, 189
Justin Martyr.......... 109

Keane John J.......... 21
Kennedy................ 216
Kenrick, Arch., 49, 56, 210, 211, 221
Kincaid, A. J........... 99
Kitto..................64, 68
Knapp, George C....... 154
Kyriasko, Prof.......... 199

Labbe and Cossart, 167, 168, 172, 174
Langen, Joseph......... 130
Lascarides, G. P........ 21
Law of baptism......... 7
Le Clerc................ 52
Leo, Rabbi............. 42
Lexicons, statement of.. 16
Libanius... 27
Liddell and Scott, 16, 17, 89, 92
Liddon, Canon.......... 103
Lingard, Dr. John...... 79
Liturgies and Missals... 176
Livy................... 30
Lucian................. 26
Luther, Martin, 37, 52, 158, 210

Mabillon............... 206
Maclaren, Dr.......... 59
Maimonides.........41, 69
Mallett................ 142
Mariott................ 202
Marshall, Chief Justice... 10

Mattes................. 207
Martini............176, 179
Maury, Bonet G.... 133, 202
Methodists, The........ 233
Meyer........ 48, 52, 67, 105
Michaelis.......... 240, 243
Milton, John... 37, 38, 93, 189, 190
Minerva, The........... 195
Miratori............... 206
Mishna, The............ 44
Moore, Thos............ 189
Muller, Max............ 148

Naaman, Baptism of.. 36, 47, 49, 92, 110
Neale, John Mason...... 245
Neander.......54, 59, 80, 153
Neo-Cæsarea, Council of. 156
Nestor................. 81
Newman, Cardinal...... 148
Nicene, Council of...... 167
Nismes, Council of...... 174
Nöldeke, Th............ 249
Noyes 65, 87

O'Farrel............... 75
Olshausen 50, 66
Onkelos................ 38
Oosterzee, Prof. J. J...... 107
Origen................. 111
Othelon................ 79
Otto, Bishop........... 80
Ovid...............138, 139
Oxford, Council of...... 173

Paciandi, Paul Maria.... 205
Paine, Prof. L. L........ 131
Parkhurst 37
Passow................. 17

INDEX.

Pastor of Hermas....110, 125
Patrick, St............ 74, 75
Paul, Baptism of........ 89
Paulinus, Arch........ 78, 79
Perthes................ 73
Philo................25, 125
Pierce Plowman........ 183
Pindar.................. 23
Plato.................. 23
Platon, Bishop.......... 197
Plotinus................ 26
Plumptre.......... 54, 66, 97
Plutarch............ 25, 26
Poets, The............. 182
Pollok................. 184
Polyænus.............. 26
Polybius.......... 24, 32, 183
Pope.............. 185, 186
Pope, Dr. W............ 19
Porphyra.............. 27
Pothier................ 11
Potter, Bishop Henry C. 21, 53
Powell, Dr. W. D.... 200, 231
Prague, Council of...... 174
Presbyterians, The...... 223
Prescott............... 144
Priesthood of Christ.... 57
Proclus................ 28
Purification, Theory of.. 58

Ravenna, Council of. 134, 174, 204
Reading, Council of..... 173
Remingius........... 76, 177
Riddle, Dr............. 122
Robinson......17, 20, 52, 63, 90
Romanus, Ordo.......... 178

Salmasius,............. 155
Sarum, Manual...... 178, 214
Saxon Visitation........ 180
Scapula................ 20
Schaff................. 37
Schaff, Dr..119, 120, 121, 130, 134, 159, 162, 180, 201, 230
Schindleri............. 37
Schleusner............. 20
Schoettgenius.......... 20
Schrevellius........... 20
Seneca................ 30
Septuagint........... 36, 87
Shakespeare........... 30
Simplicius............. 29
Simonis............ 20, 37
Smith, Bishop.......... 220
Smith, R. Payne.....244, 248
Sophocles, E. A..18, 196, 200
Sprinkling, a heathen custom, 136; history of, 158 ; many nations, 85; France first country where practiced, 160; introduction into England.............. 163
Stanley, Dean, 60, 81, 128, 134, 147, 157, 164, 180, 200, 217
Starkie................ 13
Stephanus 19, 65
Stephen, Pope.......... 153
Stockius 20, 37
Stourdza...,........... 197
Strabo..............24, 33
Strabo, Walafrid........ 134
Stuart, 21, 37, 39, 50, 110, 116, 202

INDEX.

Suicer.................... 20
Summers, Thos. O...... 71, 94
Syriac, The, 240; Ritual, 177
Syrus, Ephraim......... 245

Tables, baptism of...... 67
Talmage, Dr............ 60
Talmud, Jerusalem...... 40
Taylor, Bishop Jeremy... 60
Targum................. 38
"Teaching of the Twelve Apostles,"............. 119
Tertullian............114, 117
Thayer, J. H., 17, 18, 32, 34, 65, 90, 92
Themistius............. 27
Three thousand, baptism of, 71; Not all baptized in one day, 71; Examples of the baptism of thousands......... 73
Timayennis............. 198
Tischendorf............ 67
Todd, Dr..............74, 75
Toledo, Council of...... 168
Toy, Dr. C. H.......... 246
Trench................. 92
Tribur, Council of...... 171
Trine immersion........ 117
Trumbull, Dr.......... 59
Turretin............... 227

Use of Words..........8–12

Valesius............... 155
Venema................ 155
Vicecomes, Dr......... 206
Virgil........30, 138, 185, 186
Vladimir.............. 81
Vulgate............... 52

Wahl.................. 19
Wall, Dr....160–162, 165, 178, 201, 213, 215
Watson, Dr............ 235
Watts................. 185
Webster............... 39
Wescott..............65, 67
Wesley, John, 38, 104, 233–236
Westminster, Assembly of Divines........... 225
Westminster, Council of. 172
Wheatley...........179, 217
Williams, Sir M.....139, 141
Wise, Rabbi Isaac M..42, 47
Witsius..............35, 45
Worcester, Council of... 172
Worms, Council of...... 171

York, Council of....... 172

Zacharias, Pope,....... 79
Zwingli............... 233

A BIOGRAPHICAL SKETCH OF JOHN TYLER CHRISTIAN (1854-1925)

BY

JOHN FRANKLIN JONES

A Biographical Sketch of John Tyler Christian (1854-1925)

John Tyler Christian—pastor, professor, and historian—was born at Lexington, Kentucky December 14, 1854. The son of Marion Washington and Amanda Martinie Christian, he received both the B.A. and M.A. degrees at Bethel College, Russellville, Kentucky. He traveled to Europe seven times to do postgraduate work.

Christian was ordained in 1876. He held pastorates at First Baptist Church, Chattanooga, Tennessee (1883-86); East Baptist, Louisville, Kentucky (1893-1900); Second Baptist Church, Little Rock, Arkansas (1904-11); First Baptist Church, Hattiesburg, Mississippi (1913-19), et al. He served as Secretary of Missions in Mississippi and later in Arkansas.

He was chairman of an informal conference of friends in Houston, Texas, who met in 1915 to consider founding a theological seminary at New Orleans, Louisiana. Later, he served as chairman of a special committee to bring a recommendation concerning that institution to the Southern Baptist Convention in 1917.

Christian served as professor of Christian History and librarian at Baptist Bible Institute, New Orleans (1919-25) and traveled repeatedly in Europe and the Near East studying and collecting books. He donated his personal library of over 15,000 volumes to Baptist Bible Institute. He was a member of the Society of Christian Archaeology of Greece, the Academy of History of France, the Academy of Science, Arts and Belles Lettres of the Mediterranean, and the American Society of History.

He authored *Close Communion* (1892); *Americanism, or Romanism, Which?* (1895); *Did They Dip? An Examination of the English Baptists* (1897); *Baptist History Vindicated* (1899); *Baptism in Sculpture and Art* (1907); *A History of the Baptists* (1923); and *History of the Baptists of Louisiana* (1923). Christian died December 18, 1925, at New Orleans, Louisiana.

BIBLIOGRAPHY

Encyclopedia of Southern Baptists (1958 ed.). S.v. "Christian, John Tyler," by J. Wash Watts.

BY JOHN FRANKLIN JONES
CORDOVA, TENNESSEE
JULY 2004

THE BAPTIST STANDARD BEARER, INC.

a non-profit, tax-exempt corporation
committed to the Publication & Preservation
of the Baptist Heritage.

CURRENT TITLES AVAILABLE IN
THE BAPTIST *DISTINCTIVES* SERIES

KIFFIN, WILLIAM A Sober Discourse of Right to Church-Communion. Wherein is proved by Scripture, the Example of the Primitive Times, and the Practice of All that have Professed the Christian Religion: That no Unbaptized person may be Regularly admitted to the Lord's Supper. (London: George Larkin, 1681).

KINGHORN, JOSEPH Baptism, A Term of Communion. (Norwich: Bacon, Kinnebrook, and Co., 1816)

KINGHORN, JOSEPH A Defense of "Baptism, A Term of Communion". In Answer To Robert Hall's Reply. (Norwich: Wilkin and Youngman, 1820).

GILL, JOHN Gospel Baptism. A Collection of Sermons, Tracts, etc., on Scriptural Authority, the Nature of the New Testament Church and the Ordinance of Baptism by John Gill. (Paris, AR: The Baptist Standard Bearer, Inc., 2006).

CARSON, ALEXANDER	Ecclesiastical Polity of the New Testament. (Dublin: William Carson, 1856).
BOOTH, ABRAHAM	A Defense of the Baptists. A Declaration and Vindication of Three Historically Distinctive Baptist Principles. Compiled and Set Forth in the Republication of Three Books. Revised edition. (Paris, AR: The Baptist Standard Bearer, Inc., 2006).
BOOTH, ABRAHAM	Paedobaptism Examined on the Principles, Concessions, and Reasonings of the Most Learned Paedobaptists. With Replies to the Arguments and Objections of Dr. Williams and Mr. Peter Edwards. 3 volumes. (London: Ebenezer Palmer, 1829).
CARROLL, B. H.	*Ecclesia* - The Church. With an Appendix. (Louisville: Baptist Book Concern, 1903).
CHRISTIAN, JOHN T.	Immersion, The Act of Christian Baptism. (Louisville: Baptist Book Concern, 1891).
FROST, J. M.	Pedobaptism: Is It From Heaven Or Of Men? (Philadelphia: American Baptist Publication Society, 1875).
FULLER, RICHARD	Baptism, and the Terms of Communion; An Argument. (Charleston, SC: Southern Baptist Publication Society, 1854).
GRAVES, J. R.	Tri-Lemma: or, Death By Three Horns. The Presbyterian General Assembly Not Able To Decide This Question: "Is Baptism In The Romish Church Valid?" 1st Edition.

	(Nashville: Southwestern Publishing House, 1861).
MELL, P.H.	Baptism In Its Mode and Subjects. (Charleston, SC: Southern Baptist Publications Society, 1853).
JETER, JEREMIAH B.	Baptist Principles Reset. Consisting of Articles on Distinctive Baptist Principles by Various Authors. With an Appendix. (Richmond: The Religious Herald Co., 1902).
PENDLETON, J.M.	Distinctive Principles of Baptists. (Philadelphia: American Baptist Publication Society, 1882).
THOMAS, JESSE B.	The Church and the Kingdom. A New Testament Study. (Louisville: Baptist Book Concern, 1914).
WALLER, JOHN L.	Open Communion Shown to be Unscriptural & Deleterious. With an introductory essay by Dr. D. R. Campbell and an Appendix. (Louisville: Baptist Book Concern, 1859).

For a complete list of current authors/titles, visit our internet site at:
www.standardbearer.org
or write us at:

he Baptist Standard Bearer, Inc.
NUMBER ONE IRON OAKS DRIVE • PARIS, ARKANSAS 72855
TEL # 479-963-3831   *FAX # 479-963-8083*
EMAIL: Baptist@centurytel.net   http://www.standardbearer.org

Thou hast given a standard to them that fear thee; that it may be displayed because of the truth. — Psalm 60:4

www.ingramcontent.com/pod-product-compliance
Lightning Source LLC
Chambersburg PA
CBHW021806220426
43662CB00006B/196